The teachings of an ancient Hebrew sage, the Assembler of Wisdom, come to life

"No matter how certain you are that you are a member of the select few who will make it to heaven or nirvana or wherever it is you think you can go to escape the grave, you are never certain enough. Doubt stalks you like a shadow; the more light you seek, the more shadow you create. What if there is no exit, no escape from the impermanence of life and the finality of death? This is the koan at the heart of the Book of Ecclesiastes.... Ecclesiastes is not about the afterlife or how to escape the inevitability of death. It is about reality—wild, raw, and impermanent."   —from the Preface

Also Available in the SkyLight Illuminations Series

The Art of War—Spirituality for Conflict 978-1-59473-244-7
Bhagavad Gita 978-1-893361-28-7
The Book of Mormon 978-1-59473-076-4
Dhammapada 978-1-893361-42-3
The Divine Feminine in Biblical Wisdom Literature 978-1-59473-109-9
Embracing the Divine Feminine 978-1-59473-575-2

The End of Days 978-1-59473-170-9
Ethics of the Sages: Pirke Avot 978-1-59473-207-2
Ghazali on the Principles of Islamic Spirituality 978-1-59473-284-3
Gnostic Writings on the Soul 978-1-59473-220-1
The Gospel of Philip 978-1-59473-111-2
The Gospel of Thomas 978-1-893361-45-4

Hasidic Tales 978-1-893361-86-7
The Hebrew Prophets 978-1-59473-337-5
The Hidden Gospel of Matthew 978-1-59473-038-2
The Infancy Gospels of Jesus 978-1-59473-258-4
Lost Sayings of Jesus 978-1-59473-172-3
The Meditations of Marcus Aurelius 978-1-59473-236-2

Native American Stories of the Sacred 978-1-59473-112-9
Perennial Wisdom for the Spiritually Independent 978-1-59473-515-8
Philokalia: The Eastern Christian Spiritual Texts 978-1-59473-103-7
The Qur'an and Sayings of Prophet Muhammad 978-1-59473-222-5
Rumi and Islam 978-1-59473-002-3
The Sacred Writings of Paul 978-1-59473-213-3

Saint Augustine of Hippo 978-1-59473-282-9
The Secret Book of John: The Gnostic Gospel 978-1-59473-082-5
Selections from the Gospel of Sri Ramakrishna 978-1-893361-46-1
Sex Texts from the Bible 978-1-59473-217-1
Spiritual Writings on Mary 978-1-59473-001-6
Tanya, the Masterpiece of Hasidic Wisdom 978-1-59473-275-1

Tao Te Ching 978-1-59473-204-1
The Way of a Pilgrim 978-1-893361-31-7
Zoh... 978-1-893361-51-5

these ...oks, ... website, www.skylightpaths.com.

Rabbi Rami Shapiro, a renowned spiritual teacher, is an award-winning storyteller, poet, and essayist. He is author of *The Sacred Art of Lovingkindness: Preparing to Practice; The Divine Feminine in Biblical Wisdom Literature: Selections Annotated and Explained; Ethics of the Sages:* Pirke Avot—*Annotated and Explained; Hasidic Tales: Annotated and Explained; The Hebrew Prophets: Selections Annotated and Explained; Tanya, the Masterpiece of Hasidic Wisdom: Annotated & Explained* (all SkyLight Paths); and other books.

Rev. Barbara Cawthorne Crafton is an Episcopal priest and the author of many books. She heads The Geranium Farm, an online institute for the encouragement of spiritual growth, at www.geraniumfarm.org.

"Wisdom from beyond traditional theology.... Offers roadside assistance to the people on the ever-changing path."
—**RABBI ZALMAN SCHACHTER-SHALOMI**,
co-author, *Jewish with Feeling* and *A Heart Afire*;
author, *First Steps to a New Jewish Spirit*

Sky Light Illuminations

Offers today's spiritual seeker an enjoyable entry into the great classic texts of the world's spiritual traditions. Each classic is presented in an accessible translation, with facing pages of guided commentary from experts, offering readers the keys they need to understand the history, context, and meaning of the text. The series enables readers of all backgrounds to experience and understand classic spiritual texts directly, and to make them a part of their lives.

Walking Together, Finding the Way®

SKYLIGHT PATHS®
PUBLISHING

www.skylightpaths.com
Find us on Facebook®
Facebook is a registered
trademark of Facebook, Inc.

Ecclesiastes

Other Books in the SkyLight Illuminations Series

The Art of War—Spirituality for Conflict: Annotated & Explained

Bhagavad Gita: Annotated & Explained

The Book of Common Prayer: A Spiritual Treasure Chest—
Selections Annotated & Explained

The Book of Job: Annotated & Explained

Celtic Christian Spirituality: Essential Writings—Annotated & Explained

Confucius, the Analects: The Path of the Sage—Selections Annotated & Explained

Desert Fathers and Mothers: Early Christian Wisdom Sayings—Annotated & Explained

Embracing the Divine Feminine: Finding God through the Ecstasy of Physical Love—
The Song of Songs Annotated & Explained

Ghazali on the Principles of Islamic Spirituality: Selections from The Forty
Foundations of Religion—Annotated & Explained

The Gospel of Thomas: Annotated & Explained

The Hebrew Prophets: Selections Annotated & Explained

The Hidden Gospel of Matthew: Annotated & Explained

Hildegard of Bingen: Essential Writings and Chants of a Christian Mystic—
Annotated & Explained

The Imitation of Christ: Selections Annotated & Explained

John & Charles Wesley: Selections from Their Writings and Hymns—
Annotated & Explained

Julian of Norwich: Selections from Revelations of Divine Love—Annotated & Explained

Maimonides—Essential Teachings on Jewish Faith & Ethics: The Book of
Knowledge & the Thirteen Principles of Faith—Annotated & Explained

The Meditations of Marcus Aurelius: Selections Annotated & Explained

Native American Stories of the Sacred: Annotated & Explained

Philokalia: The Eastern Christian Spiritual Texts—Annotated & Explained

Perennial Wisdom for the Spiritually Independent: Sacred Teachings—
Annotated & Explained

Proverbs: Annotated & Explained

The Qur'an and Sayings of Prophet Muhammad: Selections Annotated & Explained

The Sacred Writings of Paul: Selections Annotated & Explained

Saint Augustine of Hippo: Selections from Confessions and Other Essential Writings—
Annotated & Explained

Saint Ignatius Loyola—The Spiritual Writings: Selections Annotated & Explained

The Secret Book of John: The Gnostic Gospel—Annotated & Explained

Sex Texts from the Bible: Selections Annotated & Explained

Spiritual Writings on Mary: Annotated & Explained

Tao Te Ching: Annotated & Explained

The Way of a Pilgrim: The Jesus Prayer Journey—Annotated & Explained

Zohar: Annotated & Explained

Ecclesiastes

Annotated & Explained

Translation & annotation by Rabbi Rami Shapiro

Foreword by Rev. Barbara Cawthorne Crafton

Walking Together, Finding the Way®
SKYLIGHT PATHS®
PUBLISHING

Ecclesiastes: Annotated & Explained

2016 Quality Paperback Edition, Second Printing

For information regarding permission to reprint material from this book, please mail or fax your request in writing to SkyLight Paths Publishing, Permissions Department, at the address / fax number listed below, or email your request to permissions@skylightpaths.com.

Translation, annotation, and introductory material © 2010 by Rami Shapiro
Foreword © 2010 by Barbara Cawthorne Crafton

Library of Congress Cataloging-in-Publication Data
Bible. O.T. Ecclesiastes. English. Shapiro. 2010
Ecclesiastes : annotated & explained / translation and annotation by Rami Shapiro ; foreword by Barbara Cawthorne Crafton. — Quality pbk. ed.
p. cm. — (Skylight illuminations series)
Includes bibliographical references and index.
ISBN 978-1-59473-287-4 (quality pbk. : alk. paper) 1. Bible. O.T. Ecclesiastes—Commentaries. I. Shapiro, Rami M. II. Title.
BS1473 2010
223'.805209—dc22

2010029510

ISBN 978-1-59473-335-2 (eBook)
ISBN 978-1-68336-041-4 (hc)

Manufactured in the United States of America
Cover design: Walter C. Bumford III
Cover art: Photo ©iStockphoto.com/Bartosz Hadyniak

SkyLight Paths Publishing is creating a place where people of different spiritual traditions come together for challenge and inspiration, a place where we can help each other understand the mystery that lies at the heart of our existence.

SkyLight Paths sees both believers and seekers as a community that increasingly transcends traditional boundaries of religion and denomination—people wanting to learn from each other, *walking together, finding the way*.

SkyLight Paths, "Walking Together, Finding the Way," and colophon are trademarks of LongHill Partners, Inc., registered in the U.S. Patent and Trademark Office.

Walking Together, Finding the Way®
Published by SkyLight Paths Publishing
www.skylightpaths.com

Contents ☐

Foreword   vii

Preface   ix

Introduction   xv

About the Translation   xxvii

Chapter One   3

Chapter Two   13

Chapter Three   27

Chapter Four   39

Chapter Five   47

Chapter Six   55

Chapter Seven   61

Chapter Eight   73

Chapter Nine   81

Chapter Ten   91

Chapter Eleven   99

Chapter Twelve   105

Epilogue (Chapter Twelve, Continued)   109

Bibliography   113

Foreword ☐

Rev. Barbara Cawthorne Crafton

Like many of my generation, I had a secular introduction to the Book of Ecclesiastes in 1965—the Byrds' hit version of Pete Seeger's musical setting of its third chapter, which we knew as "Turn, Turn, Turn." I don't know when I realized that it came from *the Bible*, of all places. I don't think we used to read Ecclesiastes in church when I was a child, not that I recall. Of course not; nobody was in the market for futility and meaningless then. Nobody in church, anyway. Not in public worship, anyway. We were all up for happy endings.

Because we wouldn't have understood the book at all. Reading it in our King James Bibles—*Vanity of vanities, saith the Preacher, vanity of vanities; all is vanity*—we would necessarily have concluded that here was a book about the meaninglessness of life. Here was a book about futility, if ever there was such a book. Teenagers in the midst of their seasons of angst sometimes found a resonance in what they thought was the book's cynicism, a quality highly esteemed among many bright, young people. If we had thought it through, we might have said the Preacher was an ancient version of T.S. Eliot, the bleak bard of our era's intellectuals, which was certainly what we all aspired to become. Less sophisticated Christians—but not much less—would even have thought that Ecclesiastes was a book about how hopeless life is without Jesus.

And there I left it. For years. Continued to love the song; still have a recording of Pete singing it. Went to seminary and remember a professorial mumble to the effect that the Preacher may have known of the cynics; that learning traveled along with merchandise throughout the Hellenistic world; that you could often pick up some Diogenes along with your Greek olives and purple cloth; that there was only one possible explanation for the book: it comes from a Greek influence. It's not really Jewish.

And no, I guess it's not. Or at least, it's not any more Jewish than it is anything else. But it arose from squarely within the community that, regardless of how different a book it was from anything else they chose, saw fit to include Ecclesiastes in its canon of holy writ, along with all the other writers for whom every misdeed was punished and every good deed rewarded, in which every ending, whether happy or not, had to *make sense*. It belongs to the whole of humanity, and in it we find what some in every culture have found: how to live our lives. Ecclesiastes is not a book about futility. It's not a book about hopelessness. Anything but. It's a book about ephemerality. It's a clear-eyed book about reasonable and modest hope in the face of the indisputable fact that the world and everything in it is always—*always*—passing away.

This I did not know until I had read Rami Shapiro's new translation and his notes accompanying it. I put it down and sighed contentedly, with that sense of homecoming I get when someone has told me a truth I was holding back on telling myself.

Preface ☐

From the moment of your birth you begin to die. There is no cure for death; no escape; no exit. If you are alive, you are going to die—today perhaps, tomorrow for certain.

Death itself, however, is not the problem. The dead have no problems. The problem is that you aren't dead yet. You are alive, and life is the problem—life lived in the shadow of eternity, under the illusion of immortality. This is the problem: you live and you want to live forever, but you can't.

Of all the cultural creations of humankind, only one solves the problem of life, and that is religion. The entire purpose of religion is to put your fear of death to rest. If you belong to the right religion and adhere to the right version of that religion, you will not die.

Yes, of course, your body will cease to function, decompose, and become compost for some other life forms, but you are not that body. You are something else, something more, something eternal. You know this to be true because no matter what changes the body endures, the "I" remains. This "I" is you. Or so you insist. And as long as you insist this "I" is you and this "I" is permanent, then there is hope.

Different religions offer hope in different ways; reincarnation and eternal life in heaven or hell are the two most common ways of escaping death. It doesn't really matter which you prefer, since both offer you the illusion of an undying "I," an "I" that you can claim is you.

You can call this "you" *atman* or soul; you can claim as the Hindu may that *atman* is ultimately Brahman, that the soul is really God, or you can claim as the Jew and the Jain do that the soul is a separate reality with its own eternal life. Along with Christians and Muslims you can imagine that this soul is rewarded or punished based on whatever system of judgment you imagine your God to support. And none of it matters at all. All that matters is that you don't die. You—the egoic you that you know yourself to be, the personality you claim is identical with the "I" you imagine yourself to be—will live on. Even Buddhism, whose founder seemed to deny the very idea of a permanent self in his doctrine of *anatman* (no self), promotes the idea of reincarnation.

Yet despite all these religious claims to the contrary, death still haunts you. No matter how certain you are that you are a member of the select few who will make it to heaven or nirvana or wherever it is you think you can go to escape the grave, you are never certain enough. Doubt stalks you like a shadow; the more light you seek, the more shadow you create. What if there is no exit, no escape from the impermanence of life and the finality of death? This is the koan at the heart of the Book of Ecclesiastes.

The Dance of Life and Death

Koans are those baffling puzzles Zen masters put to their students. The purpose of a koan is to burn through the notion that you can reason your way to wisdom and awakening. The aim of all koans is to fry your rational mind, to exhaust your capacity to create verbal hideouts behind which to escape the inevitability of death, and in this way to realize the reality of your own impermanence.

This is the koan that is the Book of Ecclesiastes: How do I live well in the face of impermanence, a state of continual emptying, unknowing, and uncertainty? You cannot answer this as an observer. You can only glimpse the answer in the midst of your life—this moment, or perhaps this one. Or to borrow from Zen master Hillel, "If not now, when?" (*Pirke Avot* 1:4). Ecclesiastes is not about the afterlife or how to escape the inevitability of death. It is about reality—wild, raw, and impermanent.

The world revealed in Ecclesiastes is an impermanent world of continual emptying. Ecclesiastes calls this *hevel*. Trying to grasp something in this world, trying to hold on to anything in this world, leaves you breathless, exhausted, and anxious. This impermanence is the nature of nature, and because this is so, the world lacks surety and certainty; change and the unknowing that change carries with it are the hallmarks of life. In Ecclesiastes you spend no time longing for escape from impermanence, but rather learn to live well in the midst of it. This is what the Book of Ecclesiastes wants to tell us. This is why it was written. This is why it is still read some twenty-five hundred years later.

Living with the Impossibility of Escape

The bulk of the Book of Ecclesiastes is an examination of life without escape. It offers no alternative to impermanence, and hence it is profoundly nonreligious. Religion is all about escape, but what you really want to escape from is inescapable—it is yourself. As long as there is an "I" seeking salvation, redemption, enlightenment, heaven, nirvana, or surrender, there is no salvation, redemption, enlightenment, heaven, nirvana, or surrender. The more you struggle, the stronger the "I" becomes and the tighter the noose of despair grips your every living moment.

You cannot understand the Book of Ecclesiastes merely by reading it or even studying it closely. Studying the text is not a waste of time, but just another way to pass time. It is just one more thing to do when you know that doing it will get you nowhere. You only understand Ecclesiastes when you live the truth its author perceives: the truth of endless emptying, *havel havalim*; no escape, the truth that there is nowhere to go and nothing to get, only this moment to live.

With this, Ecclesiastes is a spiritual text that belongs to no religion. It never mentions *YHVH*, the God of the Jews; it is unconcerned with tribal custom or priestly ceremony. It never speaks of the Hebrew Bible or the commandments and customs observant Jews use to inform their lives with tradition and holiness. It simply looks at what is, and responds. It is in this way that Ecclesiastes is a spiritual book and its author is a spiritual sage: he recognizes the compulsion to transcend the "I" and escape the reality of impermanence, and he points out the impossibility of doing so. Then, when all hope has been ripped from you, he offers a living response to the reality of impermanence that makes surrender and escape unnecessary.

While in no way referencing the Book of Ecclesiastes, Japanese Zen master Shin'ichi Hisamatsu (1889–1980) speaks powerfully to its spiritual program:

> [Only] when we truly come to be thus thoroughly cornered, this dilemma is broken through and a new functioning emerges. If, however, we are not truly cornered, this new functioning will not appear.... If we truly penetrate the existential koan ... we can, in a single stroke, awaken to the true self.
>
> (IN ANTINOFF, *SPIRITUAL ATHEISM*, P. 94)

The true self isn't something other, something permanent, something beyond or within. It is reality itself, what the author of Ecclesiastes calls *HaElohim*, "The God." When you realize you are not other than this, there is no dilemma; you cease to cling to life and at last begin to live.

How do you live? What is Ecclesiastes' prescription for living well in impermanence? Eat simply, drink moderately, work constructively, and cultivate love and friendship with two or three others. In this the wisdom of Ecclesiastes is similar to that of the tenth-century Chinese Ch'an (Zen) master Ta-sui Fa-chen:

> When asked, "When life-and-death has come to you what do you do?" he answered promptly, "When served tea, I take tea; when served a meal, I take a meal. I am afraid some people might take this to be beside the point. But, on the contrary, this hits the bull's eye."
>
> (IBID., PP. 136–37)

As you will learn in the third chapter of Ecclesiastes, life is a series of moments each with its own truth and rationale. The only thing to do is to live them as they arise. When it is a moment to cry—cry. When the moment calls for laughter—laugh. Do not anticipate what's next or cling to what was; just engage in what is for the moment it is.

Returning to Ecclesiastes: A New Perspective

I have wrestled with Ecclesiastes for decades. The more I allow the wisdom of Ecclesiastes to shatter my illusions of certainty and permanence, the more relevant its teachings become.

When I was first introduced to the Book of Ecclesiastes, I scoured commentaries—ancient and modern, Jewish and Christian—in addition to many translations. Still, what I was hearing from Koheleth was not what I was reading in either the scholarly or popular commentaries. So I wrote my own.

The Way of Solomon was published in 2000 by HarperSanFrancisco and stayed in print for almost a decade. It passed away just prior to the closing of HarperSanFrancisco itself. Having regained rights to the book, I sought to bring it back to life through my friends at SkyLight Paths. My editor, Emily Wichland, reviewed the book but wasn't eager to reprint what I had done ten years earlier. At that time I reinvented the text, blurring the line between my understanding of what Koheleth wrote and the actual words themselves. Emily wanted a more nuanced translation, one that revealed the deeper meaning of the text without violating its actual wording. The idea delighted me. I am deeply indebted to Emily for her editorial genius and grateful to SkyLight Paths for the opportunity to share Ecclesiastes with a new audience.

I wrote *The Way of Solomon* as I turned fifty; I am writing *Ecclesiastes: Annotated and Explained* as I turn sixty. I am different, and my reading of Ecclesiastes is different and a bit more mature, experienced, and insightful. So what you hold in your hands is yet another rendition of this ancient text, truer to the Hebrew of the original, and yet no less radical for being so.

Despite centuries of commentary to the contrary, Ecclesiastes is not a depressing book. It is the most honest and hopeful book in the entire Hebrew canon. The writer of Ecclesiastes learns how to live *hevel* with dignity, meaning, love, and joy. He wants you to know what he knows and seeks to point you toward it. The Book of Ecclesiastes is designed to shatter the façade of knowing and leave you naked before the wildness of reality. And then it offers you not a way out, but a way in; a way to live well in the midst of the chaos that is the only world there is.

In this, Ecclesiastes is like other wisdom books from other times and cultures, which is why I have sprinkled my commentary with similar, but by no means exact, teachings from many of them: the Gospel of Thomas, the Bhagavad Gita, the Dhammapada, the Tao te Ching, the Qur'an and Hadith, the Meditations of Marcus Aurelius, and *Pirke Avot*. If you find yourself moved by Ecclesiastes, my hope is that you will pick up and read these other texts as well.

Introduction

I was part of a painfully polite clergy panel on "Religion and Justice," when the audience Q&A turned delightfully heated. "Rabbi, you are full of crap! You, your god, your religion—it's all crap!" The speaker, or more accurately, the screamer, identified himself as a Jew, an atheist, and a socialist.

"All you clergy types are just full of it. Enemies of the people is what you are. You get us to dream of pie in the sky while we're starving here on earth. Show me one book of your so-called Holy Bible that speaks the truth. One book! Just one and I'll shut up. Just one!"

"Ecclesiastes," I said.

"What?"

"Ecclesiastes. The Book of Ecclesiastes, written by a man called Koheleth, the Assembler of Wisdom. The most honest book in the entire Hebrew Bible. It defines God as impersonal reality. It admits that the world is unfair; that bad things happen to good people and good things happen to bad people, and that is just the way it is. It says that people with power only care about power and that they will use and abuse you when it suits them to do so. It says that politicians are corrupt, clergy are inept, and the entire system of civilization is set up to take advantage of the few at the expense of the rest. It says that life is fleeting, that everything dies and nothing lasts, and that neither power nor money nor prestige nor fame nor even wisdom will save you in the end."

"It says that life is futile," someone chimed in from the side of the room.

"No, not futile, that's a poor translation. It says life is *hevel*, impermanent. Nothing lasts. Nobody wins in the end. Not even those we take to be winners at the moment."

"Now that's an honest book," the screamer said, no longer screaming. "Life's a crapshoot."

"No," I said, "not a crapshoot. In a crapshoot there's a chance that you can win. No one wins in Ecclesiastes. Not even the house."

"Jeez," a young college-aged woman said aloud, though seemingly to herself. "What kind of Bible book is that? It leaves you without hope, for God's sake."

"On the contrary," I said. "It is a very hopeful book. In fact it's the one book in the entire Hebrew Bible that I can believe in without reservation and actually try to follow. Koheleth gives you a fourfold plan for living well in the midst of all this madness."

"So what is it?" the young woman said.

"Koheleth's fourfold plan for living well: eat simply, drink moderately, find work that gives you a sense of meaning and purpose, and cultivate a few loving friendships," I explained.

There was a pause; people expected something more, something "spiritual."

"That's it," I said. "Eat well, drink smart, do what you love, and love who you can. This isn't a plan for transforming the world, but for surviving it wisely until you die."

"*Emes*! Truth!" the screamer shouted with a newfound lightness to his voice. "I like it!"

So do I. It's why I wrote this book.

Meeting Impermanence

Ecclesiastes isn't a book that entices you with pleasant words. Most English translations of Ecclesiastes open with the words "Vanity of vanity! All is vanity!" or "Futility upon futility! All is futile!" Is it any surprise that most English readers put the book down without reading any further? Life is difficult enough as it is; who needs some twenty-five-hundred-year-old curmudgeon telling me that all my effort at living well and wisely is vain and futile? So I, like most people who even bother to pick up a copy of Ecclesiastes, put it down without a second thought.

All that changed in the spring of 1972. I was a student of religion at Smith College in Northampton, Massachusetts, having convinced both Smith and the University of Massachusetts to let me enroll full-time at the all-women's college. I was one of eight men attending class full-time at Smith. We weren't allowed to live on campus, of course. My father found me a room in a boarding house, managed by some friends of his, on the edge of town. There were two rooms for rent. I took one, and a fellow male "Smithie" took the other. We both majored in religion.

One evening my neighbor burst excitedly into my room to tell me of a phenomenal discovery revealed in a Bible class he was taking. Knowing of his interest in Taoism, the professor had mentioned that the key word in Ecclesiastes, *hevel*, most often translated as "vanity," actually means "breath" or "vapor," implying not that life is worthless but rather imper-manent and empty of any fixity. We stared at each other wide-eyed: Koheleth was the Hebrew Lao-Tzu, the Jewish Buddha!

I have no idea where this revelation took my neighbor, but it captured my attention for the rest of my life. Koheleth became my guru, and Eccle-siastes my constant companion. With a few exceptions, Koheleth's Hebrew isn't that difficult to master. I read it over and over again from the perspective of emptiness and impermanence. There were always new insights to discover. In addition, I read every English translation I could find, always saddened to see them trapped in the despair that comes when one assumes life is *hevel*/futile rather than *hevel*/impermanent. It wasn't that translators didn't know the other meaning of the Hebrew—indeed, they often mentioned it in footnotes—but they never accepted it as the lynchpin for the entire book.

For me, this was inescapable. If you really want to understand what Koheleth is saying, you have to read Ecclesiastes through the lens of impermanence. And when you do, you find a powerful guidebook for living without attachment in a world without surety and security.

The world in which Koheleth lived is like our own. It was a world of competing empires, financial upheaval, crushing poverty, and deep mistrust.

If he were to return to earth today, he would find the world far more complicated, yet no less complex. He wouldn't know what to make of the Internet, but he would not be shocked by the lies and distortions it too often promotes. He might not understand the technology behind reality television, but he would have no difficulty grasping the way it is used to distract the have-nots with spectacle while the haves plunder the planet and exploit the poor and powerless. He certainly would be in awe of how our global communications networks feed our private conversations to government spies trolling for those fomenting terror and violence against not only the state but the status quo. He might also be amused that his allusion to spies as birds circling the air eavesdropping on our most intimate conversations has found technological birth in the form of security cameras, wiretaps, and drones.

The reason the Book of Ecclesiastes still speaks to us is because its author lived in a world not unlike our own and sought to free people not unlike ourselves.

The freedom Koheleth offers us is freedom from ignorance and foolishness; freedom from the illusion of surety, security, and permanence; freedom from the mad drive to protect ourselves from the vicissitudes of life through the pursuit of money and possessions. He teaches us how to navigate the chaos of life without hiding behind a false sense of order, imposed either by ourselves, by nature, or by God. Koheleth's God isn't the regulator of chaos but the creator of it. The way of The God (*HaElohim*), as Koheleth calls reality, does not lead us out of chaos, but into it. The way of The God doesn't promise us happiness, wealth, or health in this world and doesn't even imagine a world to come. The way of The God, the way of Koheleth, is learning how to find joy in food, drink, work, partnership, friendship, and love. This is not a teaching you can afford to neglect.

Who Was Koheleth?

So who was this radical iconoclast and heretic? The opening verse of the Book of Ecclesiastes seems to claim its author is King Solomon: "The sayings of the Assembler, son of David, king in Jerusalem" (Ecclesiastes 1:1). The only son of David to become king in Jerusalem was Solomon, so Solomon is usually said to be the author of Ecclesiastes. But is this true? Not at all.

It isn't uncommon for authors to use pseudonyms, and in ancient times if you were looking to give your book instant credibility among Jews, claiming it was written by King Solomon or some other key figure in Jewish history was the way to go about doing so. So opening Ecclesiastes with this line may have been the ancient equivalent of having Oprah endorse a book today.

Why pick Solomon as your pseudonym? Because he was the wisest human in all history. This is how that happened:

When Solomon was about to become king of Israel, God appeared to him in a dream and said, "Ask and I will give you anything you request!" (1 Kings 3:5). Solomon replied, "I am Your servant called to judge this mighty nation; therefore grant me an understanding heart to judge Your people, and to discern between good and evil" (1 Kings 3:8–9).

Pleased with this request, God said to Solomon, "Because you seek wisdom and discernment rather than wealth or long life, or the death of your enemies, I will grant your request. Indeed, your wisdom and discernment will be greater than any who have lived before you, and any who come after you. And I grant what you did not request: wealth and honor throughout your life, and your reputation will trump that of all other kings. And if you do as your father David did, walk in My ways, keeping My laws and commandments, then long life, too, will I grant you" (1 Kings 3:10–14).

So to claim Solomon is Koheleth, author of Ecclesiastes, is to claim that the wisdom contained in the book is most precious and true despite the fact, or perhaps because of the fact, that it contradicts the wisdom of the rest of the Bible.

Marketing purposes aside, however, who was Koheleth? We don't know. All Ecclesiastes says, in addition to its claim that Solomon wrote it, is that Koheleth was a *chacham*, a sage (Ecclesiastes 12:9). At first glance we might conclude that Koheleth belonged to a specific class of scholar/sage who, as Koheleth often does, taught by means of proverb and parable. Yet the wisdom of these sages as anthologized in the Book of Proverbs (another text said to be written by King Solomon) is directly contradicted by Koheleth.

The Book of Proverbs sees the world clearly defined by right and wrong where the former is rewarded while the latter is punished. Koheleth, on the other hand, sees a world where hard and fast distinctions are lacking, where the good are often oppressed, where evil often triumphs, and where both saints and sinners die without any final reckoning or righting of injustice. If he was part of this scholar/sage community, he was a radical among them.

What Koheleth shares with these sages is a common methodology. He examines things based not on revelation, but on reason. He uses his own mind to fathom the ways of human life. He regularly reminds us that he "turned his heart" to examine this or that. That is to say, Koheleth consults neither priests nor other sages, neither the Hebrew Bible nor Jewish tradition, but uses his own powers of observation to see what is true.

When Did He Live?

If we don't know who Koheleth was, can we at least discern when he lived? Yes.

Given that Koheleth uses some words borrowed from the Persian, the Book of Ecclesiastes was probably written some time between 550 and 450 BCE. The Babylonian exile was over, and a minority of the Jews exiled to Babylon returned to Judah to rebuild the Temple and reclaim their religious heritage under the leadership of Ezra and Nehemiah. With the death of the last of the Jewish prophets—Haggai, Zechariah, and Malachi—leadership fell to five generations of *zugot*, pairs of scholar/judges. These were the precursors of the early Pharisees and later Rabbis.

The world of the *zugot* was very different from that of pre-exilic times. While agriculture continued to be a major economic factor, cities and global commerce attracted much notice. The Persians sought to facilitate commerce in their empire by minting coins. The daric, bearing the likeness of Darius I, was a gold coin used throughout the realm, while silver coins were minted by local leaders. These coins not only facilitated business, they became a valuable commodity in their own right. When Koheleth speaks of hoarding silver and gold coins (Ecclesiastes 2:8) and decries the love of silver coins (Ecclesiastes 5:9), he is most likely thinking of the daric and other coins.

Koheleth's audience was worldly, cosmopolitan, and engaged in the new economy of the Persian empire. His language is peppered with references to business, gain, yield, and wealth. Even though he sees the value of farmland and a good harvest (Ecclesiastes 5:8), he is not talking about the pre-exilic world of subsistence farming, but a world of privatized commerce where money was readily available, trade was global, and farmland was often held by absentee landowners.

Most likely Koheleth's world was fifth-century-BCE Jerusalem, a bustling hub of commerce devoted more to making money than observing Judaism.

> This was not a world of farming villages, but of global commerce. Theirs was a world of money, commerce, and investment. It was also a world of loans, mortgages, and foreclosures. For the ordinary citizen—the smallholder, the homesteader, the worker—there was much about which to worry, but not much about which one could be certain.... The reality of the Persian period economy is that individuals were caught in the tides of swift political and economic changes, and most people were helpless in the face of all that was happening.
>
> (Seow, *Ecclesiastes: A New Translation with Introduction and Commentary*, p. 36)

Upon his return to Jerusalem from exile in Babylonia in 445 or 444 BCE, Nehemiah, sent by the Persian king Artaxerxes I to revive the city and bring it firmly into the Persian way of governance, describes the state of the city:

In those days I saw in Judah people treading wine presses on the Sabbath, and bringing in heaps of grain and loading them on donkeys; and also wine, grapes, figs, and all kinds of burdens, which they brought into Jerusalem on the Sabbath day; and I warned them at that time against selling food.

Tyrians also, who lived in the city, brought in fish and all kinds of merchandise and sold them on the Sabbath to the people of Judah, and in Jerusalem. Then I remonstrated with the nobles of Judah and said to them, "What is this evil thing that you are doing, profaning the Sabbath day? Did not your ancestors act in this way, and did not our God bring all this disaster on us and on this city? Yet you bring more wrath on Israel by profaning the Sabbath."

When it began to be dark at the gates of Jerusalem before the Sabbath, I commanded that the doors should be shut and gave orders that they should not be opened until after the Sabbath. And I set some of my servants over the gates, to prevent any burden from being brought in on the Sabbath day.

Then the merchants and sellers of all kinds of merchandise spent the night outside Jerusalem once or twice. But I warned them and said to them, "Why do you spend the night in front of the wall? If you do so again, I will lay hands on you." From that time on they did not come on the Sabbath. And I commanded the Levites that they should purify themselves and come and guard the gates, to keep the Sabbath day holy.

(NEHEMIAH 13:15–22, NRSV)

In Koheleth's world of international commerce, coins had replaced land as the means of value. People had to hire themselves out for money in order to feed themselves and their families. And when work was insufficient to meet a person's needs, debt was accrued. Again, listen to Nehemiah:

There were also those who said, "We are having to pledge our fields, our vineyards, and our houses in order to get grain during the famine." And there were those who said, "We are having to borrow money on our fields and vineyards to pay the king's tax. Now our flesh is the same as that of our kindred; our children are the same as their children; and yet we are forcing our sons and daughters to be slaves, and some of our daughters have been ravished; we are powerless, and our fields and vineyards now belong to others."

I was very angry when I heard their outcry and these complaints. After thinking it over, I brought charges against the nobles and the officials; I said to them, "You are all taking interest from your own people." And I called a great assembly to deal with them, and said to them, "As far as we were able, we have bought back our Jewish kindred who had been sold to other nations; but now you are selling your own kin, who must then be bought back by us!" They were silent, and could not find a word to say. So I said, "The thing that you are doing is not good. Should you not walk in the fear of our God, to prevent the taunts of the nations our enemies? Moreover I and my brothers and my servants are lending them money and grain. Let us stop this taking of interest. Restore to them, this very day, their fields, their vineyards, their olive orchards, and their houses, and the interest on money, grain, wine, and oil that you have been exacting from them." Then they said, "We will restore everything and demand nothing more from them. We will do as you say." And I called the priests, and made them take an oath to do as they had promised.

(NEHEMIAH 5:3–12, NRSV)

Despite Nehemiah's efforts, the people still knew extreme poverty and debt, and the wealthy continued to focus on accumulating riches in hopes of staving off any future financial collapse. Those who could not pay their debts were arrested and placed in work camps. The economy was volatile. There was no security. A person's fortunes could quickly turn upside down:

See what I have seen: that the madness of this world is so deeply ingrained that it might as well be law; that fools rise to power, and the once wealthy dwell in slums; that former slaves ride fine horses, and former financiers walk barefoot like slaves.

(ECCLESIASTES 10:5–7)

There was no middle class in Koheleth's time, only rich and poor. And while neither condition was necessarily permanent, things certainly favored the wealthy. A letter from the same time period etched on a pottery shard reveals the hardship so many labored under. The author of the letter writes home to his family: "If you will sell all my valuables, the babies may eat. There are no more coins left!" (Seow, *Ecclesiastes*, p. 34).

Similar texts speak of the failure of the justice system to protect the rights of the poor.

> Behold! The tears of the oppressed flow without ceasing, and power rests in the hands of the oppressor, and there is no one to comfort the poor.
>
> (ECCLESIASTES 4:1)

People did whatever it took to survive, and the wealthy flaunted the law wherever possible. The legal and political systems were corrupt, and the rich did whatever they pleased at the expense of whomever they wish.

In such a world there is always fear of revolution. The rich oppress the poor, who in turn scheme against them. To secure their power the wealthy instituted a system of spies forever on the lookout for plotters. So thick was the world with people willing to sell one another out to the authorities that Koheleth warns against trusting anyone, even your lover:

> Yet don't even fantasize about revolution, or curse the rich even in the privacy of your bedroom, for spies circle overhead like parrots, repeating your words and betraying you.
>
> (ECCLESIASTES 10:20)

Koheleth lived in a world much like our own. We too live in a world dominated by global commerce. We too focus on wealth and gain. We too find privacy scarce. We too worry about losing what we have, and we too are haunted by the notion that no matter how much we have it never seems to be enough. Our world, no less than his, is uncertain and unfair. His world is our world. His worries are our worries. His search for meaning is our search for meaning. His doubts are our doubts. But are his conclusions our conclusions? This is the question you must ask yourself as you read and ponder his teachings. For me, the answer is an unequivocal "yes." Koheleth's wisdom is no less valuable today than it was twenty-five hundred years ago. His portrait of life is accurate, and his suggestions as to how to find joy in the midst of such madness no less cogent. Ecclesiastes is a book for our time as well as his.

About the Translation

Every work of translation is, by its very nature, a work of interpretation. The translator cannot help but filter the original text through his or her own understanding, creating, if not an entirely new work, at least an intrinsically interpretive one. If this were not so, we wouldn't have so many different translations of the same book.

This is certainly the case with *Ecclesiastes: Annotated and Explained*. I have read and rendered the teachings of Koheleth as I understand them; and while I have studied many other translations and commentaries, I have found that none of them, not even my own, is definitive. The best way to study Ecclesiastes is to read many versions, delve into the Hebrew original as best you can, and come to your own conclusions.

I have done my best to minimize the use of Hebrew terms in my annotations, preferring instead to focus on the meaning of the text for our time. However, if you do compare this translation with others, and if you do seek out the key Hebrew words associated with Ecclesiastes, I offer the following look at these key words. In this way, you will better be able to identify my own interpretive biases and better equipped to measure them against the biases of other translators and their translations.

The Continual Emptying of Life: *Hevel*

Hevel is *the* key word in Ecclesiastes. Koheleth uses the word thirty-eight times in the Book of Ecclesiastes, slightly more often than it is used in all other books of the Hebrew Bible combined, and every understanding of Ecclesiastes depends on what we imagine he means by it.

Most translations render *hevel* as "vanity," having Koheleth open his book with "Vanity upon vanity; all is vanity" (Ecclesiastes 1:1). But this is an interpretive reading rather than a translation of *hevel*. *Hevel* means "breath" or "vapor." It is used to imply impermanence and the continual emptying of life one moment into the next. A more accurate but not yet deep enough reading of Ecclesiastes' opening line is this: "Breath upon breath; everything is mere vapor!" How did we get from "breath" to "vanity"?

The Talmud, the anthology of Rabbinic teachings from the last centuries BCE to the fifth century CE, tells us that King Ptolemy II Philadelphus, king of Egypt (287–247 BCE), in an effort to enrich the holdings of the library at Alexandria, took seventy-two Rabbinic sages, housed each in a private room, and requested of each that he translate the Five Books of Moses, the Hebrew Bible, into Greek. The Talmud goes on to say that God directed the heart of each translator so that each produced a Greek version of the Hebrew Bible identical to the others, thus proving that the Greek Bible was the work of God and not the rabbis themselves (*Megillah* 9a–b).

The rest of the Bible was translated by different hands from the third to the first centuries BCE. The resulting Greek Bible came to be called the Septuagint, a Latin word meaning "seventy," in deference to the Jewish sages (minus two) who translated the Five Books of Moses.

The Septuagint's rendering of *hevel* is *mataiotes* (mat-ah-yot'-ace), a Greek word meaning "emptiness," "purposelessness," "futility," and "transience." In 382 CE Pope Damasus I commissioned Jerome to create a definitive Latin translation of the Gospels. From 390 to 405 CE Jerome, then living in Bethlehem, took it upon himself to produce a Latin translation of the entire Hebrew Bible. This became the basis for the Latin Vulgate Bible. When translating the opening lines of Ecclesiastes, Jerome chose *vanitas* (emptiness, valueless) as the Latin equivalent of *hevel*, and in so doing stripped *hevel* of its sense of impermanence and transience that the Greek *mataiotes* had maintained. It has been *vanitas* ever since: *Vanitas vanitatum dixit Ecclesiastes, vanitas vanitatum omnia vanitas* ("Vanity of vanity," says Koheleth, "vanity of vanities, all is vanity").

Koheleth, however, was not writing in Greek or Latin. His language was Hebrew, and his understanding of *hevel* rested on other uses of the word in other biblical books. For example, Psalm 144 tells us that humanity is "like a breath" (*hevel*) and their days a passing shadow (Psalm 144:3–4). Humans are transient beings, not worthless ones. In fact, the psalmist makes it clear that God is preoccupied with humans (Psalm 144:3) despite the brevity of our lives, not despite the futility of our existence.

Limiting *hevel*/breath to *vanitas* implies that somehow breath is futile, vain, and worthless. But this is nonsense; breath is the basis for our very existence. If we failed to breathe, we would fail to live. Yet if Koheleth is simply saying that breath is essential to life, he is saying nothing of great import. But he is saying something important. Koheleth is saying life is like a breath in that it is brief, impermanent, and empty of any lasting substance. Like breath, life is impossible to grasp or hoard. Like breath, life cannot be controlled or maintained solely by the will to live. While some can hold their breath far longer than others, none can cease breathing for long without either dying or being forced to gasp for air by the body's own compulsion to live. On the other hand, no one can continue to breathe indefinitely. Eventually we all cease breathing and die, whether or not we wish this to be so.

To say life is *hevel* is to say that it is fleeting, impermanent, uncontrollable, and driven by forces beyond our will. To say life is *hevel* is to say that it is empty of security, surety, and permanence. What is vain is to think otherwise. What is futile is to live as if you could impose permanence and order on the impermanent and constantly changing. What is worthless is all talk and effort that set you against the natural flow of life.

In this translation of Ecclesiastes, I understand *hevel* as "emptying" and "impermanence," and most often translate it along these lines. I prefer the gerund "emptying" to the noun "emptiness" because the latter implies a fixed state, while *hevel* denies any permanence to things at all. To speak of "emptiness" as a noun implies there is something called emptiness toward which one can point. But this is not the case. There is no such thing as emptiness, only the never-ending process of emptying.

In addition to "emptying" and "impermanence" there is another meaning of *hevel* that I also employ, and that is "absurd." This translation comes from Hebrew scholar and commentator Michael Fox, who uses the term as others use "vanity," that is, to define all life as one thing: absurd.

While I find Dr. Fox's notion of *hevel* as "absurd" insightful, it is so only when applied to actions performed in opposition to the fundamental impermanence of life or to observations of life's irony. In other words, it is absurd to pursue profit as if we could hold on to anything in a world defined by continual emptying. Life itself offers up absurdities when it allows the wicked to prosper and the righteous to suffer. In both cases the absurdity is such only when played out against a background of fixedness and surety. It is only when we insist that life should be good, fair, just, and the like, can we speak of life being absurd for not living up to our ideas and ideals.

The truth is that life is emptying, vaporous, impermanent, committed to nothing and no one; simply arising and falling, and making room for both joy and horror.

Understood this way, Ecclesiastes isn't a condemnation of life as worthless, and human effort as vain and futile, but rather a revelation into the impermanence of reality and a guide as to how to live in the midst of impermanence and insecurity with a modicum of joy and tranquility. The genius and daring of Koheleth is that he doesn't deny the impermanence of life or offer you a way to escape from it. There is no escape. What he does offer, and what makes the Book of Ecclesiastes so vital, is a way to live well in the midst of life's continual emptying.

The God, Absolute Reality: *HaElohim*

Life is *hevel*—forever emptying and impermanent, often absurd, and ultimately beyond our ken and control. Why is this so? Because *HaElohim*, "The God," made it so. With only a couple of exceptions, Koheleth refers to God as "The God," *HaElohim*, rather than the simple *Elohim*, "God," found in the rest of the Hebrew Bible. Koheleth never mentions the ineffable name *YHVH*, the four-letter Name of God used over six thousand times in the Hebrew Bible and typically translated as "Lord."

Some might be inclined to translate *HaElohim* literally as "the gods," but such a reading would require a plural verb to justify a plural reading of the noun, and this Koheleth does not supply. Despite the plural suffix *-im*, it is clear from his grammar that Koheleth has but one deity in mind. But who is this God?

It certainly isn't the anthropomorphic God of the Hebrew Bible who walks in the Garden, talks with His creation, and intervenes time and again in the affairs of individuals and nations. Koheleth's God is ungendered, highly abstract, and distant. The God, Koheleth tells us, transcends life on earth (Ecclesiastes 5:1), a very different position than that offered in Deuteronomy, "So acknowledge today and take it to heart that the Lord is God in heaven above and on the earth beneath; there is no other" (Deuteronomy 4:39).

It is The God who sets the universe in motion, who is responsible for its quality of impermanence, and who allows for justice and injustice, good and evil, joy and sorrow. While it is The God who creates the world in such a manner as to allow humans to discover how best to live with the reality of continual emptying, this discovery is not in any way the product of supernatural or divine revelation. On the contrary, it is the result of reasoned analysis: "I disciplined my mind to wisdom, investigating all that happens under the sky" (Ecclesiastes 1:13).

Our capacity to investigate and discover the truth of *hevel* and how best to live with it is also natural. The God created a world that would eventually come to know itself, and human beings are a means for this knowing. Yet all knowing is contingent on the moment rather than definitive: "Everything is beautiful in its moment, but the ripening is hidden from your mind, and you cannot comprehend beginnings or endings" (Ecclesiastes 3:11). So there is no end to our investigations.

Who then is *HaElohim*? If you really want to get a glimpse into Koheleth's understanding of The God, I suggest you shift from speaking of God as "who" and refer to The God as "what." "*Who*" implies that God is a person of some sort, or if not a person at least a personality.

"*What*" suggests that God is an impersonal force, the absolute reality that shapes the relative world you and I experience every day.

This "what" may be hinted at in the Book of Deuteronomy. Referring to the horrors God inflicted on the Egyptians during the Hebrew people's exodus from Egypt, the Hebrew Bible says, "You have been shown [all this] in order to know that *YHVH* is *HaElohim*! There is none other than that" (Deuteronomy 4:35). Here the author of Deuteronomy asserts that *YHVH* is The God, clearly giving preference to *HaElohim* over *YHVH*. In other words, the Hebrew Bible isn't saying that *HaElohim* is *YHVH*, Israel's God, but that *YHVH* is *HaElohim*; Israel's God is the far more abstract and cosmic *HaElohim*. This, I suggest, is why Koheleth doesn't refer to *YHVH* at all, and only to *HaElohim*. Koheleth isn't writing for Jews alone, and he isn't offering a Jewish theology. He is speaking about reality in its most cosmic sense and thus chooses the Hebrew noun that reflects this: *HaElohim*.

Koheleth's God isn't *YHVH*, the God of Israel, or even *Elohim*, the creator of heaven and earth (Genesis 1:1), but *HaElohim*, The God who embraces and transcends them both. *HaElohim* is beyond human imagination and categories of thought. Right and wrong, good and evil, justice and injustice are human inventions; *HaElohim* transcends these, and reality as *HaElohim* establishes it often ignores and distorts them, and there is nothing we humans can do about it.

In writing this, Koheleth may have the older Book of Job in mind. Job's friends Bildad and Elihu insist God never distorts justice, and the good always reap just rewards, while the wicked always suffer (Job 8:3, 34:12). Job himself insists otherwise (Job 19:6) and demands that God explain why this is so. While Koheleth agrees with Job that The God allows for the distortion of justice, he simply accepts the fact as it is and never asks that it be other than it is. Job's God, called *Elohim*, is a being with whom Job can meet. Koheleth's The God is beyond all that.

While careful not to take the analogy too far, it may be helpful to say that *HaElohim* is closer to the Chinese understanding of Tao than the classical Jewish, Christian, or Muslim notion of God.

The Tao embraces and transcends all reality and yet can be experienced and lived as a "way." The Tao is not a person who wills, but reality itself giving rise to all things and their opposites. You don't worship Tao nor ask favor of it; you simply investigate the way and learn to walk it wisely. This is what Koheleth does and what I suspect he means by *HaElohim*.

It is with all this in mind that I render the Hebrew *HaElohim* as "reality" and "life." Koheleth isn't talking about a god or deity, but about reality, the very nature of nature, the source, substance, and way of all things. Ecclesiastes isn't a theological tract, but a rational examination of the way of life as you and I experience it.

The Effort of Living: *Ahmahl*

Life has to be lived, and living it is *ahmahl*, "effort" or "toil." Koheleth often speaks of effort negatively, but this is only in regard to effort that is fueled by ignorance of *hevel*, or toil aimed at overcoming impermanence. For example, if you devote your life to stockpiling money and goods in hope of gaining security, you will fail. There is no security in life. If you toil to achieve some sense of immortality or permanence, this too is a waste of effort and time. We all die, and in time we are all forgotten. Yet this is not to say that Koheleth rejects all effort. On the contrary, he tells us that we can find true joy in doing what we love with those we love. Effort in tune with *hevel* brings joy. Effort in opposition to *hevel* brings only bitterness and frustration.

Wisdom as a Verb: *Chochma*

Chochma, "wisdom," appears fifty-two times in Ecclesiastes. Wisdom is often juxtaposed with folly, and the wise with the foolish. Wisdom is an alternative to folly, but not an alternative to *hevel*. Wisdom doesn't offer you an escape from impermanence, but rather reveals a way to navigate it. Koheleth takes pains to make it clear that the wise and the foolish meet the same fate, that is, they all die. Wisdom doesn't guarantee you political power or financial success, and there are numerous cases where the wise suffer unjustly while the foolish seem to prosper.

Yet wisdom is preferable to folly when used as a navigation tool. When you are wise, you know the nature of *hevel*. When you understand the nature of *hevel*, you cease to toil against it. When you cease all effort in opposition to impermanence, you are free to live wisely with impermanence.

Wisdom, then, isn't a body of fixed knowledge, but a way of investigating reality and how best to live with it.

Reaping the Consequences of Living: *Heleq*

Heleq, or "portion," refers to a person's lot in life. Your lot is not predestined in the sense that you are simply the passive victim of fate. Rather it means that at each moment of life you reap the consequences of earlier moments and the actions taken in them. In Koheleth's world everything is created with its opposite, and both will be encountered over time. This is the meaning of the wonderful poem in chapter 3 where we are told there is a season for everything under heaven: birth and death, love and hate, war and peace. To cling to any one of these in hopes of avoiding its twin is absurd, for it denies the essential nature of reality: *hevel*. Given a long enough life, you will experience joy and grief, connection and loss. To live expecting anything else is absurd. Your portion in life is life with all its impermanence.

A Vexed Spirit: *Re'ut Ruach/Ra'yon Ruach*

The idioms *re'ut ruach* and *ra'yon ruach* are closely linked to *hevel*, "breath." *Ruach* is another Hebrew word for "breath," as in the opening verses of Genesis where we are told that *ruach Elohim*, "the breath of God," fluttered over the waters (Genesis 1:2). *Re'ut* and *ra'yon* both mean "troubling" or "vexation." Hence *re'ut ruach* and *ra'yon ruach* mean "a disturbing of the breath" or "a vexation of the spirit." This is a far cry from the more poetic, but less accurate, rendition "chasing after wind" found in the New Revised Standard Version of Ecclesiastes or the Jewish Publication Society's translation as "pursuit of wind."

These more conventional renderings hearken back to the mistaken notion of *hevel* as "futility." What could be more futile than trying to chase after wind? But when we understand *re'ut ruach* and *ra'yon ruach* to mean "a troubling of the breath," we see a perfect parallel with *hevel*: life is like breath, and actions taken in violation of this truth—that is, actions designed to freeze life or grasp something permanent in a completely impermanent universe—are only going to upset your breathing. You will either huff and puff, needlessly laboring to do the impossible or gasp in horror when your best efforts and plans give way to the impermanence of life.

Koheleth wants to teach you how to live with *hevel* with a sense of tranquility, that is, without *re'ut ruach* and *ra'yon ruach*. And when you do live this way, the result is joy.

Re'ut ruach and *ra'yon ruach* strike me as Hebrew parallels to the Buddha's notion of *dukkha*, "dissatisfaction" or "disease." *Dukkha* is one of the three marks of existence along with *anicca* (impermanence) and *anatta* (no separate self). When we live in ignorance of the impermanence of all things, including oneself, we live life in a way that produces suffering and dissatisfaction, a vexation of mind, breath, and spirit.

The Buddha speaks of three kinds of *dukkha*. The first, *dukkha-dukkha*, is the suffering that arises from pain, illness, old age, death, and grieving over the dead. The second kind of *dukkha* is *viparinama-dukkha*, the suffering caused by our insistence that life meet our expectations, despite the fact that all expectations violate the truth that life is unconcerned with our desires. The third form of *dukkha* is *sankhara-dukkha*, psychological dissatisfaction arising from our inclination to cling to things, people, and ideas.

When you live in ignorance of impermanence—what the Buddha calls *anicca* and what Koheleth calls *hevel*—you live in a manner that cannot help but produce dis-ease, anxiety, and a troubling of your breath and spirit. The solution isn't to escape from the fact of impermanence, but to learn to live wisely within it. For Koheleth this means eating simply, drinking moderately, working meaningfully, and cultivating love and friendship.

The Joy of the Moment: *Simcha*

The Book of Ecclesiastes is a guide to *simcha*, "joy." Not permanent joy, for there is no permanence, but the only joy a person can experience in this life—fleeting but no less satisfying joy. When we wrongly imagine that Koheleth hates life and decries the value of all effort, we can't imagine why he might speak of joy at all. But when we realize that he is leading us to joy by first freeing us from the illusions of surety, security, and permanence that plague our lives, then we can see how helpful and positive a vision he is really offering.

There is no joy in efforts made to overcome *hevel* because impermanence cannot be overcome. Such efforts can only bring *re'ut ruach* and *ra'yon ruach*, a troubling of your breath. But there is joy in effort made in sync with *hevel*. Knowing that death is inevitable, and all too soon, leads the sage to find joy in daily life, no matter how difficult that life may be. Knowing that working in hopes of securing a trouble-free retirement is useless, you are free to find work you enjoy, even if low paying. Knowing that all relationships end frees you to find joy in the moments before they end. Knowing that there is no guarantee that you will have food to eat tomorrow frees you to enjoy the food you have today.

Koheleth's use of *simcha* is well defined in a delightful Zen story:

A man was walking through the forest and unintentionally fell into a pit dug to trap a tiger. At the bottom of the pit were sharpened bamboo spikes placed there to skewer the tiger and kill it. The man managed to grasp hold of a vine growing along the side of the pit and thus avoid the fate set for the tiger. Before he could hoist himself up the vine and out of the pit, however, the tiger arrived. The trap being sprung, the tiger peered into the pit and saw his next meal.

The man would now have to cling to the vine and wait for the tiger to grow bored and leave. Just then a mole dug his way out of the side of the pit where the vine hung and began to gnaw his way through it. The man's fate was sealed. If he quickly climbed out of the pit, he would be killed by the tiger. If he held on to the vine, the mole would weaken it and he would fall on the spikes and die. Death was imminent and unavoidable. Just then the man noticed a strawberry growing out of the vine. He plucked the strawberry, popped it into his mouth, and exclaimed, "This is the best strawberry I have ever eaten!"

This is the *simcha* Koheleth offers us. Death and tragedy are unavoidable, but futility is only present if you imagine there should be a way out. There is no way out of *hevel*, and free from false hope and an endless and vain search for an exit, you can experience reality as it is: grieving over the losses and enjoying every strawberry you come across.

The World of Impermanence: *Tachat HaShemesh*

Tachat hashemesh, literally "under the sun," is a recurring phrase in Ecclesiastes. It refers to the world of *hevel*, the world you and I know and engage with daily. Some take the phrase to imply that there is another world, a world above the sun, an afterlife in which permanence is experienced as eternity and immortality. This is a huge stretch and requires the reader to twist Ecclesiastes into knots. Nowhere does Koheleth speak of an afterlife or any refuge from *hevel*. Ecclessiastes isn't about escaping this world, but about learning to live in it wisely, in a manner that calms the breath and offers true, if temporary, joy.

"Under the sun," *tachat hashemesh*, there is only impermanence, insecurity, unknowing, and a continual emptying of things, sometimes into their opposites and sometimes into nothing at all. There is nothing above the sun, no life beyond this life, no world other than this world, nothing outside reality. So if you want any sense of joy and purpose at all, find satisfying work, and eat, drink, and rejoice with friends.

The Awe in God-Fearing: *HaElohim Yirah*

HaElohim yirah, "fear The God," is troubling because we see "fear" as a purely negative thing. We fear others because we suspect they mean us harm. If we fear God, are we saying that God, too, in some way means us ill? Rather than answer the question, some commentators, myself included, often leap at the fact that *yirah* also means "awe," so we avoid the question by removing the catalyst. We don't fear God: we are in awe of God.

Fair enough, but not far enough. In a world defined by *hevel*, the continuous emptying of all things; in a world where love can turn to hate without warning; where war can shatter peace no matter how long established, isn't fear a legitimate stance?

The key to understanding *yirah* as either fear or awe is to remember that Koheleth is referring to *HaElohim*, The God beyond all gods and theologies. *HaElohim* is the source of *hevel*, not its conqueror. We stand in awe of *HaElohim* because we are in awe of *hevel*. We stand in fear of *HaElohim* because we know that our lives and our fortunes could be lost at any moment.

When Koheleth tells us to fear The God and obey The God's commandments (Ecclesiastes 12:13), we must not think in Rabbinic terms and imagine that Koheleth is urging us to follow Rabbinic law and custom. There were no rabbis in Koheleth's day, and since Koheleth makes no mention of the Hebrew Bible whatsoever, he cannot be talking about any dictates found in or foisted upon it.

If all that matters is to adhere to some fixed set of prohibitions and prescriptions, the Book of Ecclesiastes is irrelevant, and all Koheleth's searching completely unnecessary. But the book isn't irrelevant, and the searching is necessary, because *HaElohim* is the very source of *hevel*, and the commandments Koheleth is referring to are the practical insights he has discovered for living in *hevel* with joy.

God-fearers, then, are those who know they do not know and who make no effort to grasp a fixed meaning and purpose of life. God-fearers stand in awe of the unknowability of life, and yet because they understand *hevel*, they know how to navigate it. The opposite of God-fearers are fools who imagine that there is some surety to be grasped and some security to be had. Fools, Koheleth tells us, live in perpetual ignorance, refusing to light a candle in the dark, insisting instead that stumbling blindly will eventually bring them to a place of eternal light.

The Profit in Impermanence: *Yitron*

Throughout our text, Koheleth asks, "what *yitron*" can you derive from life and your efforts in life? *Yitron* is usually translated as "profit," in the sense of something being left over after all is said and done. The word appears only in the Book of Ecclesiastes and is often used to remind us that there is no profit to things at all. This is not a negative comment or proof of the worthlessness or futility of human existence.

On the contrary, Koheleth is simply saying that the value of action is in the action itself and not the result, for the result cannot be predetermined and is always temporary. For example, what profit, in the sense of something left over, is there in burning a candle in the dark? None if we expect that something of value remains when the candle burns down and the flame sputters out. But this doesn't mean there was no value while the candle was aflame. While nothing has permanent profit, many things can profit us in the moment.

Ecclesiastes

1 The Hebrew here is *Koheleth*. Derived from the root *k-h-l*, "to gather or assemble," Koheleth is not a name but a title.

2 This appellation leads traditionalists to assume that Koheleth is King Solomon. But since Ecclesiastes was written some four centuries after Solomon, this is doubtful. Koheleth sought to enhance his teachings by linking them with King Solomon, a common practice in ancient times.

3 This is the key Hebrew phrase of the entire book—*havel havalim!*—repeated and expanded just two words later, *havel havalim hakol* ("all is") *hevel*. While most translations render it as "Vanity upon vanity; all is vanity" (KJV, NRSV) or "Utter futility! All is futile!" (JPS), *hevel* also means "insubstantial," "impermanent," "vaporous," "as empty and as transient as breath." Koheleth's message isn't that life is vain or futile, but rather that it is transient and empty of permanence. Ecclesiastes is a guidebook to living without permanence, surety, and security while still finding joy in living.

~ "Look upon the world as you would on a bubble. Look upon it as a mirage." (Dhammapada 13:4)

~ "All conditioned things are impermanent. The one who knows and perceives this fact ceases to be miserable. This is the way to purity of vision." (Dhammapada 20:5)

~ "Jesus said: One who knows everything else but who does not know himself knows nothing." (Gospel of Thomas, logiaon 67)

4 *Tachat hashemesh*, under the sun, refers to this world of impermanence, *hevel*. Is there a life above the sun, beyond this world? Koheleth makes no mention of it. His concern is not with metaphysical speculation, but with the nature of this world and how to live wisely in it.

Chapter One

1:1
The sayings of the Assembler,[1]
son of David, king in Jerusalem:[2]

1:2
Emptying upon emptying!
—said the Assembler—
Emptying upon emptying!
Everything is emptying.[3]

1:3
A lifetime of labor under the sun,
and yet what survives?[4]

5 What would happen if the sun rose and set but once? Or if the winds blew in one direction only? Or if the sea actually filled up? Life as we know it would end. Nature requires *hevel*. What is true of nature is true of you as well. You are not on a journey from point "A" to point "B." The goal isn't to arrive, but to meander, to saunter, to make your life a holy wandering.

~ "The Tao is empty; when utilized, it is not filled up. So deep! It seems to be the source of all things." (Tao te Ching 4)

~ "Behold! In the creation of the heavens and the earth, and the alternation of night and day, there are indeed signs for people of understanding." (Qur'an 3:190–91)

6 Koheleth is referring to babble designed to mask the emptying of life behind a flood of words. To mask impermanence, you talk endlessly of souls, the afterlife, reincarnation, and karma.

7 Seeing and hearing are acts of continual emptying, *hevel*. You cannot see "this" until you stop seeing "that"; you cannot hear new sounds if your ears continually ring with old sounds. Koheleth is telling you that clinging is dying, and emptying is living, for life is ceaseless change. Seeing and hearing are all about change, while exhausting talk is all about clinging to the words of the past no matter how out of sync with truth they may be.

~ "Is anyone afraid of change? What can take place without change? What then is more pleasing or more suitable to the universal nature?" (Meditations of Marcus Aurelius 7:18)

1:4
The earth outlasts you,
and humanity passes away
one generation after another.

1:5
The sun rises only to set,
and then races breathless
to the place of rising once again.

1:6
The wind spins without end,
one moment southward,
the next moment northward.

1:7
All rivers empty into the sea,
yet the sea never fills;
indeed the waters rise and return
to the river's mouth
that they might flow yet again.[5]

1:8
Talk exhausts us,
and eventually we fall silent;[6]
yet the eye never tires of seeing,
nor the ear of listening.[7]

8 Time is cyclic. Like the rising, setting, and rising again of the sun, nothing is once and for all, but rather over and again.

⌢ "Returning is the movement of the Tao." (Tao te Ching 40)

⌢ "[Jesus said:] If they ask you, "What is the sign within you of your Father?" reply to them, "It is movement. It is rest." (Gospel of Thomas, logiaon 50c)

9 This world is *hevel*: just this arising and just this dissolving. The universe is simply a dance of "on" and "off" or, to borrow from the binary language of computers, "ones" and "zeros." A certain configuration may be new to you, but its essence is not.

⌢ "All things are the same, familiar in experience, and ephemeral in time, and worthless in the matter. Everything now is just as it was in the time of those whom we have buried." (Meditations of Marcus Aurelius 9:14)

10 What is lost or forgotten is the truth of *hevel*, the continual emptying of all things.

11 You crave permanence and hence invent immortality. You imagine that immortality is personal: you won't die; you will live forever in eternity, hellish or sublime. When the idea of personal immortality no longer makes sense to you, you imagine a more humanistic immortality: others will remember you. Koheleth wishes to free you from all fantasies of permanence. You will die and in time so will everyone who ever knew you. As long as you cling to the notion of immortality you will fail to embrace the preciousness of this mortal existence, this very moment.

12 This is another verse seeking to identify Koheleth with King Solomon, a historic impossibility. I have taken it to mean that Koheleth was rich *like* a king and not literally a king himself.

1:9
Life is an endless round:
what has been will be,
what has been done
will yet be done again.[8]
There is nothing new beneath the sun.[9]

1:10
Even that which surprises
—Look! Something new!—
is only that which has been lost or forgotten.[10]

1:11
And just as you forget the past,
so the future will forget you.[11]

1:12
I, the Assembler,
lived like a king in Jerusalem.[12]

13 Koheleth lays no claim to revelation or divine insight. His wisdom comes from a disciplined mind willing to observe reality rather than take refuge in fantasy. You can test the wisdom of Koheleth by investigating matters for yourself.

14 What I translate as "reality" Koheleth calls "The God," *HaElohim*. The God isn't the anthropomorphic deity of this or that sect or theology. It has no special people or land, no temple or form of worship, and offers no special revelation. The God is reality itself. Reality asks nothing from anyone and offers everything to everyone.

Reality has but one desire—to express itself; and but one goal—to know itself. Life speaks to the former; consciousness speaks to the latter. Despite the discomfort consciousness engenders in us, we are nevertheless driven to seek out the truth, to investigate the nature of things, to face the truth of *havel havalim*, the continual emptying of all things.

15 Koheleth looks unflinchingly at life, and what does he discover? *Hevel*! Emptiness, impermanence.

16 The Hebrew here is *re'ut ruach*. The Jewish Publication Society translates this as "pursuit of wind," while the New Revised Standard Version has "chasing after wind." *Ruach* can be rendered as "wind," but it also means "spirit" and "breath." *Re'ut*, however, doesn't mean "chasing" or "pursuing," but rather "upsetting" or "vexing." Koheleth is telling you that when you examine the nature of things and find nothing of permanence, you are troubled and your breathing is vexed—rapid and shallow, as when you are afraid. Seeing things as they are, yet wanting them to be other than they are, troubles your breath and robs you of tranquility. The key is to accept things as they are—in a state of constant emptying. In this way you will not chase after the illusion of permanence or immortality, but find joy in the fleeting nature of life.

17 Reality is reality, and there is nothing you can do to change that, and all your efforts to do so only vex you further.

1:13
I disciplined my mind to wisdom,
investigating all that happens under the sky.[13]
How troubling this obsession with knowing
that reality implants in our minds![14]

1:14
I have examined everything
done beneath the sun
and—behold!—
it is all fleeting and impermanent,[15]
leaving you anxious and disturbed.[16]

1:15
There is no straightening
of the twisted,
no making something out of nothing.[17]

1:16
I said to myself:
"My wisdom surpasses
all my predecessors in Jerusalem,
my mind is well acquainted
with theories and facts."

18 Koheleth isn't saying that wrong thinking upsets your tranquility; he is saying that all thinking does. The more you perceive the true nature of things—their impermanence—the more troubled you become. Why? Because you desire security, and security demands permanence. If there is none of the latter, there can be none of the former, so tranquility is lost. But, as you shall see, tranquility isn't Koheleth's measure of wisdom, joy is.

1:17
I set my mind to knowing
wisdom and folly and even madness,
and all of it left me gasping and vexed.

1:18
With great wisdom
comes great anxiety;
increase knowledge
and you increase pain.[18]

1 Koheleth doesn't condemn pleasure but discovers that it, too, is impermanent and emptying. If you imagine that pleasure will give meaning to life, you will be sorely disappointed. Meaning only has meaning if it is permanent or at least leads to permanence. But there is no permanence, only *hevel*. So hedonism offers you no hope. But then neither does asceticism. Indulging pleasure or denying pleasure, neither affords you any lasting hope.

~ "There is no satisfying lusts, even by a shower of gold pieces. The one who knows that lusts have a short taste and cause pain is wise." (Dhammapada 14:7)

2 The Hebrew *lischok*, "laughter," is best understood as mockery. Often the last refuge from absurdity is irony and mockery. While these may make you feel superior to those trapped in pursuit of permanence, they do nothing to improve the way you engage impermanence.

~ "Higher people hear of the Tao, they diligently practice it. Average people hear of the Tao, they sometimes keep it and sometimes lose it. Lower people hear of the Tao, they laugh loudly at it. If they do not laugh, it would not be the Tao." (Tao te Ching 41)

3 You can deaden yourself through drink, but drunkenness isn't transformative; you cannot escape the reality of impermanence.

☐ Chapter Two

2:1
I said to myself,
"Let's experiment with physical pleasure
and see what is good,"
but this, too, yielded nothing of lasting value.[1]

2:2
Mockery, I said, is madness;[2]
and drunken revelry, too, accomplishes nothing.[3]

2:3
Yet I drowned myself in wine,
even as I devoted my heart to wisdom,
in this way testing folly against wisdom
to see which we humans
ought to pursue under the sky
during the fleeting days of our lives.

2:4
I did everything on a grand scale:
I built mansions and planted vineyards.

2:5
I made gardens and orchards
in which were planted fruit trees of every kind.

4 Koheleth left nothing to speculation. He didn't interview the wealthy; he became wealthy. He didn't observe the complaints of the rich—how their stewards and maids took advantage of them, how they worried about their flocks and their herds and their investments—he acquired vast holdings and experienced firsthand the anxiety that haunts them. There is no solace in wealth or power; only wisdom seemed to comfort him. Yet, as Koheleth will confess, even wisdom cannot overcome *hevel*, only show you how best to live with it.

2:6
I dug reservoirs to irrigate the young trees.

2:7
I bought
more field hands and house slaves,
more stewards and maids,
more cattle and sheep
than anyone who lived before me.

2:8
I hoarded coins both silver and gold,
raided the treasure-houses of kings,
and stripped caravans of their precious cargo.
I filled my homes with singers and musicians.
I piled crate upon crate
stuffed with the most prized luxuries.

2:9
I grew wealthier
than any of my predecessors in Jerusalem,
and yet none of this satisfied me,
nothing but wisdom alone.[4]

5 Note that Koheleth doesn't say he found no pleasure in luxury. On the contrary, his heart reveled in all of it! This is what makes Koheleth so convincing. He isn't an ascetic who takes no pleasure in life, but rather a person who found real joy in his indulgences.

6 What Koheleth discovers isn't that there is no joy in pleasure, but that joy is no less fleeting than everything else. One pleasure has to be replaced with another and then another. There is no end to pleasure's pursuit, and you are left panting in exhaustion, with nothing to show for all your efforts.

~ "[Jesus said:] If you do not know yourselves, then you exist in poverty and you are that poverty." (Gospel of Thomas, logiaon 3b)

7 What is the folly and madness Koheleth explored? He doesn't say, but we can speculate that he devoted himself to the distractions of his day. Had Koheleth lived today, he might have surrendered himself to Internet gaming, daytime soap operas, hyperbolic and vitriolic radio, or the voyeurism of reality television—Jerry Springer, and even Oprah.

8 Koheleth uses *melech* (king) in this verse, but since the role of an actual king has little if anything to do with instructing the people by example, I have rendered *melech* as "sage." The role of the sage is to instruct the people by word and by example. What makes Koheleth so compelling is his willingness to experiment with alternatives to wisdom to be certain that they do not in fact trump wisdom. We can trust Koheleth's insights because he tested them out for himself.

~ "The sage, whose mind is unruffled in suffering, whose desire is not roused by enjoyment, who is without attachment, anger, or fear—take him to be one who stands at that lofty level [of enlightenment]." (Bhagavad Gita 2:56)

9 Notice that while light is superior to darkness, it does not vanquish darkness. Light and dark go together; you cannot have one without the other. So too wisdom and folly; each makes sense only in conjunction with the other.

2:10
I yielded to every desire
my eyes made known to me;
I denied myself nothing.
No pleasure was taboo.
And, in truth, my heart rejoiced in it all,
and this joy was the reward
for all my accumulation.[5]

2:11
Yet when I measured this joy
against the quality of my deeds
and the energy spent in doing them,
there was no doubt that this, too, was absurd,
a useless panting,
yielding nothing of lasting value.[6]

2:12
Having tested pleasure,
I turned to folly and madness.
Perhaps these would surpass wisdom.[7]
For this is the task of the sage,[8]
to do all that can be done
that those who follow
might learn from their example.

2:13
And I discerned
that wisdom is superior to folly
the way light is superior to darkness.[9]

10 Light is superior to darkness in that it is more revealing than darkness. It is easier to navigate life in the light than in the dark. Similarly, it is easier to navigate life aided by wisdom than aided by folly. Navigating life well requires that you see the consequences of your actions and thus adjust those actions for the better. The light of wisdom illumines both the act and its consequences, while the darkness of folly leaves you blind to the implications of what you are about to do.

⌐ "Fools do not know what awaits them when they commit evil deeds, but these fools are consumed by their own deeds, as if burnt by fire." (Dhammapada 10:8)

11 Do not imagine that wisdom rescues you from *hevel* or secures you a prize after death. You die if you are wise; you die if you are foolish. There is nothing after. There is no escape from *hevel*. The wise know this and learn to live well with it. The foolish deny this and pass their days anxiously pursuing the illusion of permanence and personal immortality.

12 Wisdom, like everything else, is impermanent and fleeting. Wisdom isn't something to which to cling, but a way of seeing that allows you to navigate the wildness of life in a manner that yields meaning.

⌐ "Wise people walk on, whatever may happen. They do not speak out of desire for sensual gratification. Whether touched by happiness or sorrow, they never appear elated or depressed." (Dhammapada 6:8)

13 Why does Koheleth focus on this? To rid you of concern with the afterlife. This life is what matters—your life in this world under the sun, this world of *hevel* and inevitable death. And in this world, wisdom is more helpful than folly.

⌐ "For death is as sure for that which is born as birth is for that which is dead. Therefore grieve not for what is inevitable." (Bhagavad Gita 2:27)

2:14
Wisdom opens the eye to consequence,
while folly provides no discernment.[10]
And yet the wise and the foolish
share the same reward—death.[11]

2:15
So I said to myself,
 "If the fool's fate is the same as mine,
has wisdom any lasting advantage?"
And I concluded that
wisdom, too, was empty,[12]

2:16
for in the end
both wise and foolish are forgotten.
The death of one is identical
to that of the other![13]

14 This is hyperbole, for as we shall see, Koheleth doesn't hate life. He is in fact trying to show you how best to live it. What he hates is all your efforts to overcome the state of impermanence, for these distract you from reality and rob you of any chance to live well and wisely.

⤳ "He who is content without attachment, free, his mind centered on wisdom, his action, being done as a sacrifice, leaves no trace behind." (Bhagavad Gita 4:23)

15 Why exhaust yourself and labor for more than you need? To leave an inheritance for your children? They may squander everything you've amassed and be no less foolish for your efforts. Don't worry about the future. Simply do what brings you meaning, purpose, and joy right now.

⤳ "Perform all your actions with mind concentrated on the Divine, renouncing attachments and looking upon success and failure with an equal eye. Spirituality implies equanimity." (Bhagavad Gita 2:48)

2:17
I hated the living
and despised all their efforts
made beneath the sun.[14]
Nothing lasts,
everything is transient,
and all effort to the contrary
is a needless gasping for air.

2:18
I despised even my own efforts under the sun,
for whatever I owned
would pass to those who succeed me.

2:19
Who knows if they will be wise or foolish?
Yet they will control all I amassed,
though not the wisdom
that sustained me under the sun.
And yet this worry, too, is absurd.[15]

2:20
So I turned my heart away
from all my worldly labors and achievements.

2:21
Even if you labor wisely,
with intelligence and skill,
still the reward falls to those
who inherit without labor.
To wish otherwise is nonsense—
a deep and senseless troubling.

16 This question isn't rhetorical; answer it! Look at all your efforts thus far in life. Look at all the worry that haunts you. Look at all the anxiety that stalks you. What value are you deriving from living this way? Does any of your effort protect you from the death of a loved one, the loss of a job, the ending of a dream? Is there anything you do—is there anything you can do—to ensure happiness?

~ "Expecting nothing, his mind and personality controlled, without greed, doing bodily action only—though he [the sage] acts, yet he remains untainted." (Bhagavad Gita 4:21)

17 There is nothing you can do to escape the harsh reality of *hevel*. Indeed, the more you seek to pile up worldly defenses against the inevitability of death and loss, the more you rob yourself of what pleasures this world has to offer.

~ "You have only the right to work, but none to the fruit thereof. Let not then the fruit of your action be your motive, nor yet be enamored of inaction." (Bhagavad Gita 2:47)

18 This, plus the cultivation of friendship and love, is Koheleth's prescription for the good life.

~ "Remember that very little indeed is necessary to live a happy life." (Meditations of Marcus Aurelius 7:67)

~ "Like the paths of swans in the sky, the path of those who have mastered their cravings, who are moderate in what they consume, who perceive the ultimate void, and who live in complete freedom is difficult to understand." (Dhammapada 7:4)

~ "O Children of Adam ... eat and drink, without being excessive, for God does not love those who are excessive." (Qur'an 7:31)

2:22
What can you show for all your effort?
What value do you glean
from your worrisome preoccupations?[16]

2:23
Dissatisfaction arises daily,
and business is a frustration so great
that your mind cannot sleep at night.
To live this way is absurd![17]

2:24
So what isn't absurd?
To eat simply, and drink moderately,
and do work that satisfies the soul.
This is what reality offers us.[18]

19 Koheleth wants you to find wisdom and live wisely. His concern isn't with your children or grandchildren, but with you. You cannot eat or drink for the future, and you cannot survive on the eating and drinking of the past. You have to eat when hungry, and drink when thirsty, and the pleasure of doing so is yours alone.

~ "Not to blame, not to strike, to live restrained under the law, to be moderate in eating, to sleep and sit alone, and to dwell on the highest thoughts—that is the teaching of the awakened." (Dhammapada 14:7)

20 Pleasing reality—pleasing *HaElohim*, "The God," in the original Hebrew—means living in harmony with the nature of reality, *hevel*. When we live in harmony with *hevel*, with the continuous emptying of things, we live simply, wisely, and joyously.

21 To live in opposition to *hevel*, to seek to impose permanence and security in a world empty of both, is to set yourself up for great disappointment.

2:25
For who should eat and find satisfaction if not you?[19]

2:26
One who *is* pleases reality;[20]
reality grants wisdom, intelligence, and joy.
But to the hoarder addicted to things,
amassing great wealth for the future,
all that is gathered will pass to another
more in touch with reality.
So hoarding, too, is absurd and troubling.[21]

1 This is the revelation offered by the insight of impermanence. Everything is in the process of emptying. Once you abandon the idea of permanence, you are free to experience each moment arriving and falling away. Mastering wisdom, the art of living in harmony with *hevel*, means knowing this moment and acting in sync with it. When you cling to what is passing or grasp foolishly at what has yet to arrive, you are living foolishly.

~ "Rabbi Shimon ben Elazar teaches: Don't cool another's anger in the midst of rage. Don't console the bereaved while their dead lie before them. Don't question the intention of one whose vow is already made. Don't seek out a friend whose shame still stings." (*Pirke Avot* 4:23)

☐ Chapter Three

3:1
Everything in this world has its moment,
a season of ripening and falling away:[1]

3:2
Moments of birthing and moments of dying;
moments of planting and moments of reaping.

3:3
Moments of killing and moments of healing;
moments of demolition and moments of building.

3:4
Moments of weeping and moments of laughing;
moments of mourning and moments of dancing.

3:5
Moments of scattering stones and moments of gathering stones;
moments of embracing and moments of distance.

3:6
Moments of seeking and moments of losing;
moments of clinging and moments of releasing.

2 There is no thing without its opposite, and to live clinging to one without in time welcoming the other is to be a fool.

~ "Some things are hurrying into existence, and others are hurrying out of it; and of that which is coming into existence, part is already extinguished. Motions and changes are continually renewing the world, just as the uninterrupted course of time is always renewing the infinite duration of ages." (Meditations of Marcus Aurelius 6:15)

~ "Thus being and nonbeing produce each other; difficult and easy bring about each other; long and short reveal each other; high and low support each other; music and voice harmonize each other; front and back follow each other." (Tao te Ching 2)

3 Deep down you want the world to operate on your time, according to your agenda. But life isn't like that, and living as if it were only adds needless suffering to your life and the lives of those around you. Allow things to ripen as they will, and harvest them at their peak. This requires utmost attention.

4 The human affliction is denial of *hevel* and clinging to passing moments as if you can put an end to impermanence. Impermanence is the way of things. Welcome what comes, bid farewell to what goes, and the affliction is healed.

~ "Unhappy am I because this has happened to me. Not so, but happy am I, though this has happened to me, because I continue free from pain, neither crushed by the present nor fearing the future.... Remember too on every occasion that leads you to exasperation to apply this principle: not that this is a misfortune, but that to bear it nobly is good fortune." (Meditations of Marcus Aurelius 4:49)

3:7
Moments of tearing and moments of mending;
moments of silence and moments of talking.

3:8
Moments of loving and moments of hating;
moments of warring and moments of peacemaking.[2]

3:9
What's the point of being willful,
demanding to reap that which has not yet grown?[3]

3:10
I have looked deeply into this human affliction:[4]

5 The Hebrew here is *olam*, which the NRSV translates as "a sense of past and future," and JPS renders as "eternity." While *olam* can be rendered this way, it can also be translated as "hidden." Read this way, Koheleth is telling you that the flow from one moment to another happens subtly, often beneath your notice.

6 By the time you notice something arising it is already in the process of passing away. Attempts to time the beginning or ending of things are futile. Accept the fact that you cannot know what the next moment will bring or where the last moment has gone. Learn to live with unknowing.

7 Since you can neither predict nor control the flow of things, the wisest path is to engage what is without hesitation.

8 Engaging fully with each moment isn't a passive act. On the contrary, full engagement is done with the intent of bringing out the good in that moment. Bringing out the good means bringing each moment to fruition so that it can manifest what it contains and then die completely, leaving nothing in its wake.

9 Here again is Koheleth's ultimate teaching: eat simply, drink moderately, and devote yourself to work that provides you with a sense of satisfaction. Koheleth is uninterested in faith, prayer, or any otherworldly distraction. His concern is with this world alone and how best to live in it. This is what makes Ecclesiastes such a controversial book. And one we so desperately need to read and follow.

10 *Hevel* is the only constant. Change and emptying are all there is. Realizing this can leave you feeling awesome or awful. You feel awful when you try to cling to moments passed; you feel awesome when you engage a moment just at the time of ripening. Wisdom requires full attention and unhesitating engagement at just the right time. This is not an easy way to live, but it is the only way that offers you the gift of awe and wonder.

3:11
Everything is beautiful in its moment,
but the ripening is hidden[5] from your mind,
and you cannot comprehend beginnings or endings.[6]

3:12
From this I concluded
it is best for you to rejoice in what is[7]
and devote your life to goodness.[8]

3:13
This is the gift of reality:
eat and drink and find work
that pleasures your heart.[9]

3:14
Reality's flow is endless,
moment to moment nothing is added
and nothing is taken away,
and its sole purpose is to open you to wonder.[10]

11 There is nothing new under the sun because nature is *hevel*, the emptying of one thing into nothing, and nothing into something, and back again. Koheleth reminds you of this here to sharpen his urging that you not cling to the form of the moment but rest in the never-ending flow of moments.

12 This sentence literally reads, "The God [*HaElohim*] seeks the pursued." The God is not the anthropomorphic God of this or that scripture, nor the transcendent Other that you may imagine standing over and against this world. The God is reality itself, the flow of *hevel*, the rising and falling of moments. The pursued are those haunted by the past and the future, those who simply cannot be present to what is, those who imagine there is an exit, some escape from *hevel*. Reality doesn't reject these people the way a god may reject an unbeliever. On the contrary, reality confronts them and you at every turn, the way gravity confronts a stone suddenly loosed from a cliff face.

13 Don't imagine *hevel* is restricted to the natural world; civilization too is emptying and impermanent. Justice gives way to injustice and righteousness to unrighteousness the way dawn surrenders to dusk and dusk to dawn.

14 Your heart intuits the truth of *hevel*, and there is no sense in trying to impose your will and desire on the world. Rather let things be as they are, and seek to bring out the good in whatever ripens.

15 Your purpose is to see the true nature of reality, the way of *hevel*. And when you do, you are humbled, no longer capable of pretending you are other than nature, higher than animals. You and they are simply ways reality shows itself.

3:15
What is has been before;
what will be has been before;[11]
and reality seeks the pursued.[12]

3:16
There is more to observe under the sun:
justice is displaced by injustice,
and righteousness by wickedness.[13]

3:17
My heart spoke to me,
 "There is a season for everything and every deed;
let reality determine which is to ripen when."[14]

3:18
And I spoke to my heart,
 "Life has chosen humans
to see that we are beasts."[15]

16   Don't imagine that you are superior to other animals and that somehow you will rise to heaven while they descend into the earth. Humans
are formed from the dust of the earth (Genesis 2:7) and, as Abraham
says, are nothing but dust and ash (Genesis 18:27). Yet this is not
depressing, but a cause for wonder: you are dust made conscious,
dust capable of love in the face of death! It is this realization that allows
Job to take comfort in being dust (Job 42:6; see Stephen Mitchell's
translation *The Book of Job*, pp. xxxii and 128–29). The preciousness
of this is revealed to the wise and brings them joy, while the foolish
are saddened in their pursuit of illusions.

17   The single spirit is reality itself, The God (*HaElohim*) that is the source
and substance of all things and their opposites. The reason you can feel
such love for and from animals is that you share the same mind, the
same essence, the same truth—*havel havalim*. Only they don't try to
evade this truth. It is what makes their love simpler and often more
pure than your own.

18   Koheleth has no interest in heaven and hell; his concern is with this
life only. And because it is, he offers no excuse for, or escape from,
the suffering of this world. He eschews all self-serving references to
karma, fate, reincarnation, or otherworldly reward and punishment. If
you want justice, bring out the justice within you and do justly. But
know that injustice cannot be abolished.

⌐   "Jesus said: When you give rise to that which is within you, what you
have within you will save you. If you do not give rise to it, what you
do not have will destroy you." (Gospel of Thomas, logiaon 70)

19   Do you imagine you are something special? Do you pretend that
people are more precious than animals? Do you imagine some are chosen while most are not; that some are saved while others are damned?
All this is foolishness. There are no winners and losers in a world defined
by *hevel*. There are only beings living the moments allotted them.

3:19
And the fate of human
is not other than that of the beast:
as one dies, so too the other,[16]
and they all share a single spirit.
There is no elevation of human over beast,
for everything is emptying.[17]

3:20
The fate of all life is forever the same:
from dust arising to dust returning.[18]

3:21
Why imagine that human spirits ascend
while animal spirits descend?[19]

20 Yet this realization doesn't lead Koheleth to despair. On the contrary, it makes plain to him what you should be about: finding joy in your lot. You have no control over your fate, and insisting otherwise only sets you on a course of action that is both futile and vexing. So engage well whatever comes your way, knowing that there is no alternative.

➤ "Through the passage of time, verily human beings are in a state of loss, except those who have faith, and do righteous deeds, and join together in the mutual enjoining of truth, and of patient persever-ance." (Qur'an 103)

21 This moment is all you have. The next is as yet unknown. Do all you can do now, and let "then" ripen of its own accord.

➤ "No man can attain freedom from activity by refraining from action, nor can one reach perfection by merely refusing to act." (Bhagavad Gita 3:4)

3:22
So I concluded that
there is nothing better for you
than to find joy in what you are given to do,
for doing is your lot.[20]
And none can see what the future holds.[21]

1 Koheleth now takes a closer look at the way people live and finds oppression everywhere. Is his world different from your own? After three thousand years of monotheism—Jewish, Christian, Muslim—are the poor any less poor? Are the powerful any less corrupt and oppressive?

➤ "The courts are corrupt, the fields are barren, the warehouses are empty; officials wear fineries, carry sharp swords, fill up on drinks and food, acquire excessive wealth. This is called robbery. It is not the Tao!" (Tao te Ching 53)

2 This is, of course, hyperbole employed to make his point all the stronger: oppression is so rampant that only the dead escape its reach.

➤ "But as for a life of a hundred years lived viciously and unrestrained—a life of one day of virtue and self-control is better. And as for a life of a hundred years lived foolishly and wantonly—a life of one day of wisdom and rightness is better. And as for a life of a hundred years lived idly and weakly—a life of one day of diligence and strength is better. And as for a life of a hundred years lived without seeing the impermanence of all things—a life of one day of seeing the impermanence is better." (Dhammapada 8:11–14)

3 There is no escape from the necessity of labor. You need to eat, so you have to work. But why work beyond what is required for a decent life? Why allow work to push everything else to the margins? Koheleth says it is envy that drives us. Think about it: does capitalism work when envy is absent? If you didn't crave more, would you work less?

➤ "Foolish people follow after vanity. Wise people guard vigilance as their greatest treasure." (Dhammapada 2:6)

4 If excessive work isn't the key to the good life, perhaps you should opt for idleness instead. But this, too, is useless, for the idle are no less consumed by envy. Their envy of others turns into resentment, and their resentment leaves them impotent and fuming.

□ Chapter Four

4:1
I returned to my investigation
of the oppressions of this world:
Behold!
The tears of the oppressed flow without ceasing,
and power rests in the hands of the oppressor,
and there is no one to comfort the poor.[1]

4:2
Perhaps the dead are more fortunate than the living,

4:3
but if so, better still those as yet unborn,
for they have not seen the evils of this world.[2]

4:4
I considered toil and skilled labor
and found everyone driven by envy of the other.
Why huff and puff over emptiness?[3]

4:5
Yet the flesh of the fool
who folds his hands and does no labor
is no less consumed.[4]

5 The answer is moderation: work just enough to find joy in what you do and what good it brings you. Then stop. Enslaved to work, you have no time for family and friends. And without these there is no one to share the bounty of your efforts, so your success is hollow.

~ "Therefore do your duty perfectly, without care for the results; for he who does his duty disinterestedly attains the Supreme." (Bhagavad Gita 3:19)

~ "Knowing contentment avoids disgrace. Knowing when to stop avoids danger. Thus one can endure indefinitely." (Tao te Ching 44)

6 Perhaps you excuse your obsession with work by claiming that you are laboring not for yourself but for your dependents. You work so that your children will have a better life than you have. Koheleth has already told you (Ecclesiastes 2:18–19), however, that this is absurd, seeing as how you cannot know for certain that your heirs will appreciate their inheritance or use it wisely. But even more absurd are those who labor endlessly without dependents or heirs. Work is not an end but a means, and the end isn't to amass more than you can use, but to earn just enough to meet your basic needs, leaving as much time as possible for friends and family.

7 The reward Koheleth refers to is not merely financial. The reward from working with a partner is the partnership itself.

8 Koheleth builds on the notion of partnership, moving from partner to friend to lover. In all three cases he sees the value of relationship most clearly in times of trouble. When you fall—whether financially, emotionally, or even spiritually—a true friend is there to help you rise up. This is Koheleth's definition of a friend: one who is there to lift you up when you fall down. Cultivating such friendship requires time and dedication, both of which are lacking when your life is defined by excessive work.

4:6
Better to work a little in joy
than to be obsessed with work
at the expense of tranquility.[5]

4:7
I turned my attention
to another absurdity under the sun:

4:8
There are those who,
though lacking dependents,
toil endlessly in pursuit of all their eyes desire
without ever asking,
"For whom do I sacrifice happiness
on the altar of ceaseless toil?"
How absurd!
A senseless task![6]

4:9
Working with a partner
is better than working alone,
and together you earn a greater reward.[7]

4:10
And if you should fall,
your friend can lift you up.
How sad to fall alone
with none to raise you![8]

9 Koheleth may be referring to partners and even friends, huddling together against the cold, or he may be referring to yet another level of intimacy, when friends become lovers.

10 Friendship and love are central to Koheleth's view of right living. Find someone with whom to share your work and your life, someone you can rely on in times of trouble, someone with whom to share your bed at night. The stronger your bonds with others, the stronger your capacity to engage life with courage. While this degree of friendship may limit the number of deep friendships you can cultivate, Koheleth's reference to a three-ply cord is not meant to affirm three as the optimal number of friends you may have.

⌐ "Adapt yourself to the things with which your lot has been cast; and the men and women among whom you have received your portion, love them, but do it truly, sincerely." (Meditations of Marcus Aurelius 6:39)

⌐ Jesus said: If two can make peace between themselves in a single house, they can say to a mountain, "Move!" and it will move." (Gospel of Thomas, logiaon 48)

11 The Hebrew that I render as "financier" is *melech*, literally "king," but given the previous verses, I suspect Koheleth isn't talking about the politically powerful but the financially so.

12 Do not mistake caution for hesitation. You are cautious when you use wisdom to see what is ripening in the moment (Ecclesiastes 3: 1–8) and the consequences of your actions (Ecclesiastes 2:24). Wise caution allows you to act effectively. Hesitation is rooted in fear and folly: failing not only to act timely and well, but even to act at all.

⌐ "Should you wish to act, ponder well the consequences. If good, carry on; if not, desist." (Prophet Muhammad, in Sultan, *The Qur'an and Sayings of Prophet Muhammad*, p. 119)

4:11
And at night in bed,
you can warm one another,
for how does one who sleeps alone stay warm?[9]

4:12
And when alone you may be overpowered;
two can withstand an attacker,
and a three-ply cord is not easily severed.[10]

4:13
Better to be young, poor, and wise
than to be a foolish and doddering financier[11]
incapable of caution.[12]

13 People are impressed by wealth and seek to attach themselves to the wealthy. But when that wealth passes, the people fade away. Do not place your trust in youth or wealth, but in wisdom alone.

~ "Beware the powerful, their friendship is a matter of convenience. They will abandon you when it suits their purposes to do so." (*Pirke Avot* 2:3)

14 Koheleth speaks of "The God's House," *Beit HaElohim*, rather than the normative "House of God," *Beit Elohim*, the Temple in Jerusalem. Following our notion that *HaElohim*, "The God," refers to reality, *Beit HaElohim* may be the world in which you dwell moment to moment.

15 If *Beit HaElohim* refers to the world, drawing close and listening means that you should observe life carefully rather than lose yourself in the sacrifice of fools, the sacrifice of happiness, friendship, and tranquility that comes when you give in to envy and endless toil. On the other hand, if Koheleth is speaking of the Temple in Jerusalem, he is criticizing the wealthy who enter the Temple with great pomp, offering sacrifices not in service to God, but to flaunt their wealth and stature.

16 Whether Koheleth is talking about the world or the Temple, the evil is the same: a worldview that denies *hevel*, holds out the false promise of permanence, and entices you away from the only life that matters: living simply, working constructively, and cultivating loving friendships.

4:14
Even if he had risen from a debtor's prison
to the palaces of high finance,
from great poverty to extreme wealth and power,

4:15
it is the way of ordinary people
to abandon him when his wealth is gone,
and to flock to a second and more promising youth
who will take the other's place in the halls of power.[13]

4:16
There is no end to those
flocking to power and youth,
and new generations lack respect for the old.
So this, too, is absurd and upsetting.

4:17
Step carefully as you walk to The God's House;[14]
to draw close and listen is better
than to offer the sacrifice of fools[15]
oblivious to the evil they do.[16]

1 Don't place your faith in words or mistake babble for brilliance. The way of reality cannot be reduced to concepts and ideas, and all efforts to do so leave you bitter. So speak little and observe much.

⌐ "Too many words hasten failure and cannot compare to keeping quiet." (Tao te Ching 5).

2 Dreams often reflect your anxiety over *hevel*, impermanence. Your anxiety produces an endless stream of talk designed to mask the truth of *hevel*, and this gives rise to foolishness.

3 In a world where partnership, friendship, and love are central to the good life, your word is crucial. His advice is simple: say what you mean, and do what you say.

4 The Hebrew I render as "negative results" literally means the "wrath of The God." Since Koheleth avoids anthropomorphism, he cannot be referring to an angry and vindictive god. On the contrary, invoking The God's wrath means setting in motion events that can only lead to your own destruction.

☐ Chapter Five

5:1
Don't let your mouth rush to speak
or let your heart race toward bitterness;
for reality transcends your life on earth,
so keep your words few.[1]

5:2
Just as dreams arise from great worry,
so foolishness arises from too many words.[2]

5:3
When you make a vow,
do not delay completing it.
What you promise—do!
Only fools vow with no intent to follow through.

5:4
Better not to promise at all
than to promise and not fulfill.[3]

5:5
Do not let your reputation suffer because of your mouth
nor deny a promise when challenged to fulfill it.
Why invoke negative results with lies
or allow falsehood to destroy all your efforts?[4]

5 Again my naturalist rendering "be in awe of reality" is *HaElohim yirah*, which most translators render as "fear God." The Hebrew word *yirah* means both "fear" and "awe", and the latter seems more appropriate to Koheleth's understanding of The God, *HaElohim*, as reality. What he is saying is this: Reality, like the ocean, has is own current. While drowning is always a possibility when swimming in the ocean, working with the current is wiser than working against it.

6 Koheleth has no faith in government, another reason to doubt he is King Solomon.

7 The powerful protect their own, and there is no point in getting worked up over this. Time spent trying to change the system is time wasted. Better to let the system consume itself through its own madness and folly, while you focus on living well and wisely.

◄ "Love work, shun clerics, and do not get cozy with the government." (*Pirke Avot* 1:10)

8 Koheleth lived in a time when agriculture was the basis for wealth. While international traders could and did grow very rich, a single loss of a trading vessel or caravan could ruin them (Job 1:17). Real wealth is found in owning land and being able to eat of the harvest. Yet even land ownership cannot guarantee a good harvest; thus even kings are not self-sufficient, having themselves to depend on the bounty of the land.

9 Koheleth is well aware that the more you own, the more what you own owns you.

◄ "Hillel used to say: The more fat, the more disease. The more possessions, the more worry. The more wives, the more rivalry. The more maids, the more frivolity. The more butlers, the more theft." (*Pirke Avot* 2:8)

5:6
Don't get caught up in dreams,
distractions, and endless talk—
simply be in awe of reality![5]

5:7
Don't be surprised that the State
oppresses the poor and subverts justice,
for this is the nature of politics;[6]
the lower officials are protected by the higher,
and the higher are protected by those higher still.[7]

5:8
Do not be impressed by high finance,
for real wealth is in the land;
even kings are dependent upon the harvest.[8]

5:9
How absurd is the lust for silver coins.
Who can eat coins?
Hoarders of things still lack wheat.

5:10
The more you have,
the more you have to maintain;
where is the advantage in owning all you see?[9]

10 Just as Koheleth places no faith in politics, he places no faith in business either. All he sees are people worried sleepless about protecting what they have and laboring endlessly to procure more. There is no end to the envy and greed, and a life lived in subservience to these forces is a life lived in a greater poverty.

⌐ "There is no crime greater than greed; no disaster greater than discontentment; no fault greater than avarice; thus the satisfaction of contentment is the lasting satisfaction." (Tao te Ching 46)

11 This is the nature of foolishness: you sacrifice the only joy there is in world—the joy of eating simply, drinking moderately, working at something you love, and loving friends and family—in order to defeat the specter of *hevel*, only to succumb to it, leaving your children with nothing, not even your love.

12 In the end we all die, so why waste your life building fortunes?

⌐ "Jesus said: Once there was a rich man who had lots of money, and he said, 'I will invest my money so that I can sow, reap, plant, and fill up my silos with crops so that I won't lack anything.' So he thought, but that night he died. He who has ears, let him hear." (Gospel of Thomas, logiaon 63)

⌐ "My soul was saddened by the sons of men, for they are mentally blind. They do not see that they have come into the world empty and they will go out of the world empty." (Gospel of Thomas, logiaon 28)

13 We are born with nothing and we die with nothing, so why try to fill the intervening years with stuff? Koheleth isn't opposed to things or the joy things can bring, but he finds the notion that quantity rather than quality is the key to happiness not only ludicrous but at the root of all suffering.

14 "Eating in darkness": consuming without understanding; stuffing yourself without knowing the harm you are doing.

5:11
Whether they eat much or little,
sweet is the sleep of the honest worker;
but the rich toss and turn from their cravings.[10]

5:12
I have seen a great heartache in this world:
you hoard your wealth to guard against the future,

5:13
only to lose it all in a deal gone bad.
If you have children, they will inherit nothing.[11]

5:14
As you emerged naked
from your mother's womb,
so will you return;
there is nothing to salvage
from all your labor,
and nothing to hand on.[12]

5:15
What a tragic waste!
You leave as you came,
so what did you gain
from all your breathless toil?[13]

5:16
Your whole life
is spent eating in darkness,
making yourself ill with worry and anger.[14]

⌐~⌐ "Gold and jade fill up the room; no one is able to protect them. Wealth and position bring arrogance and leave disasters upon oneself." (Tao te Ching 9)

15 Again Koheleth returns to his core piece of advice: eat and drink with moderation, and find work that makes you happy. Happiness, not money, is the true wealth.

⌐~⌐ "What then is that about which we ought to employ our serious efforts? These things only: thoughts just, and acts social, and words that never lie, and a disposition that gladly accepts all that happens as necessary, as usual, as flowing from a principle and source of the same kind." (Meditations of Marcus Aurelius 4:33)

⌐~⌐ "Attain the ultimate emptiness; hold on to the truest tranquility. The myriad things are all active; I therefore watch their return." (Tao te Ching 16)

16 Good and bad, success and failure, wealth and poverty happen to whom they happen. This is simply the way of life. Avoid the needless drama of fate, karma, or divine favor or retribution. Use what you have wisely and well, and do not imagine more than reality actually allows.

⌐~⌐ "If you have some money, don't lend it out at interest, but give it to someone who will not return it to you." (Gospel of Thomas, logiaon 95)

17 What did you do with what you were given? The answer to this question is what people will remember about you when you die. Are your hands occupied with work that brings you joy? Is your heart filled with gratitude regardless of the events that befall you? Anything less is a wasting of life and an unnecessary vexing of your breath.

⌐~⌐ "He who, before he leaves his body, learns to surmount the promptings of desire and anger is a saint and is happy." (Bhagavad Gita 5:23)

5:17
So what is worthwhile?
Simply to eat and drink
and find pleasure in your daily tasks.
This is the life-way you are given.[15]

5:18
Take pleasure in whatever you receive,
no matter how much or how little;
accept what is and learn to enjoy it;
this is the gift reality offers.[16]

5:19
In this way you will not
fall prey to anxiety,
for you will be filled with joy.[17]

1 The disease Koheleth warns you about is the incapacity for joy. If you cannot enjoy what you have, having it means nothing. Joy arises from simplicity: eating simply, drinking moderately, working constructively, loving deeply. If this foundation is laid, having more or having less will not distress you. But if this foundation is lacking, if you do not know joy at all or, worse, you are so driven by the disease of greed and envy that you are never capable of the sense of satisfaction and gratitude joy requires, then your life is nothing but an exercise in futility.

⌐ "There is light within a man of light, and he lights up all of the world. If he is not alight, there is darkness." (Gospel of Thomas, logiaon 24)

☐ Chapter Six

6:1
Here is another common horror
I have witnessed in this world:

6:2
There are people to whom life grants
great riches, wealth, and good reputations—
people who possess all that their hearts crave
and yet who lack the capacity to enjoy any of it.
They die loveless;
and their wealth falls
into the hands of strangers.
How absurd and wicked a disease![1]

6:3
And then there are those
who live long lives—
though the numbers of years are not important—
and have hundreds of children,
yet if they, too, are incapable
of finding contentment in the goodness life brings,
I say the stillborn left unburied
is yet better off!

2 Koheleth's message, though hyperbolic, is clear: joy is the key to living well. But how is joy cultivated? You know the answer: eat and drink in moderation, find work that satisfies you, and cultivate love and friendship.

3 You come into the world to manifest joy, not accumulate wealth or indulge in pleasure. If you fail to manifest joy, no matter how long your life you live as if stillborn.

4 If you imagine wealth and pleasure to be the keys to joy, you will devote your life to working for these as prerequisites to joy. By the time you discover that joy has nothing to do with wealth and pleasure, you are too exhausted to be truly joyous; you are as if dead.

5 So find joy while you live. When you are content with what you have, you will naturally eat well, drink well, engage in work that is constructive and satisfying, and find friends with whom to share all these. And that is the joy you were born to encounter.

6:4
Though the stillborn lacks purpose
and dies in obscurity,
a name without deeds;

6:5
though it never sees the sun
nor reaches consciousness,
even this stillborn has more satisfaction
than those who lack the capacity for joy.[2]

6:6
Even if you could live for a thousand years
—and a thousand more—
if you live without joy you are like the stillborn,
and the one ends up in the same place as the other.[3]

6:7
You labor to satisfy your hungers,
yet your hungers never cease,
and your spirit is never satisfied.[4]

6:8
If you are clever in the ways of finance
yet lack the capacity for contentment,
are you at all superior to the financially ignorant?
Is a contented pauper less than a discontented financier?

6:9
Better to be content with what you have
than be driven to distraction by fantasies of wealth.
Striving after silly dreams is absurd
and serves only to trouble your breathing.[5]

6 You are mortal, and you will die; if not today, then tomorrow. You cannot escape this simple fact. This is what it means to see the world as *havel havalim*, emptying upon emptying. Nothing is permanent, nothing is secure, nothing is certain. And nothing you can do can alter this fact at all.

7 So how do you respond to impermanence and insecurity? Do you embrace *hevel*, or do you hide from it? Most people hide, and most of them hide in busy-ness: rushing here and there, doing this and that, grasping all they can and racing back for more when what they grasped fades like dew. Is this all there is to you? Are you more than craving and clinging, grasping and hoarding?

~ "If you do not fast from the world, you will not find the Kingdom." (Gospel of Thomas, logiaon 27a)

8 Each moment arises and falls of its own accord, and there is no knowing in advance what may be. You may do what you think is good only to find it bad, or you may observe what appears on the surface to be bad and yet as the moment ripens it turns out to be good. Surety is simply not part of this world.

~ "The saint is awake when the world sleeps, and he ignores that for which the world lives." (Bhagavad Gita 2:69)

9 Fantasies about death are at the heart of all religious systems. They are the way you avoid the absolute truth of *hevel*. You say to yourself, "Perhaps it is true that this world is marked by impermanence, but the next is surely eternal." But can you really know this? Of course not. And because you know you can't know, doubt creeps in and robs you of even this false security.

Koheleth urges you to live with not knowing. His is the wisdom of insecurity. There is little you can know in this world, and nothing you can know of any world to come. Take refuge in what can be known, and leave the rest alone. What can be known? That all life is emptying, and that to live well in an emptying world means to eat simply, drink moderately, work constructively, and befriend lovingly.

6:10
Each of us has limits;
we are all transient creatures,
and no amount of effort can change that.[6]

6:11
There are infinite ways to waste your life
and add to your frustration.
Is there nothing more to you than this?[7]

6:12
Life is short and your days are like dew.
Consider your life as a shadow,
and don't imagine you know what is good.[8]
You cannot know what will happen when you die.[9]

1 In Hebrew this is a pun: Koheleth links a fine name, *shem*, with fine oil, *shemen*.

2 Your reputation, your "name," is determined by the sum of the choices you make and the actions you take, and this cannot be known until the day you die.

⌣ "Relatives, friends, and lovers salute those who have done good and have gone from this world to the other—as kinfolk welcome dear ones on their homecoming. In like manner, one's good works bless one who has done good and has gone from this world to the other—as kinfolk welcome dear ones on their homecoming." (Dhammapada 16:11–12)

3 Are you at home with death? Have you made peace with *hevel*, impermanence and emptying? At home with death, at peace with *hevel*, you are free from anxiety and free to live fearlessly and fully.

4 Grief offers you the opportunity to slow down and reflect upon life, while gaiety too easily gives way to giddiness. When you reflect on life, you are reminded again and again that nothing is permanent, that everything is emptying. Realizing the impermanence of all things, you have compassion for all things, especially those who deny reality and exhaust themselves in the futile pursuit of permanence.

5 Facing the inevitability of your death and the death of all you love, you are almost compelled to ask yourself: Am I living the way I wish? Am I living in a way that brings joy and gladness to myself and those I meet?

6 The instruction of the wise deepens your capacity for wisdom and compassion. This is how you know their words are wise. The songs of praise gushing from fools only feed your ego and drive you deeper into self and selfishness.

☐ Chapter Seven

7:1
A fine reputation is superior to fine oil,[1]
and your last day is preferable to your first.[2]

7:2
Thus it is more advantageous
to visit a house of mourning
than a house of feasting;
for death is our common end,
and only a heart at home with death truly lives.[3]

7:3
Grief is preferable to gaiety,
bringing a reflective sorrow
that awakens compassion.[4]

7:4
Thus the heart of the wise
rests in the home of sorrow,
while the heart of the fool
clings to the house of feasting.[5]

7:5
Heeding the correction of the wise
is better than being distracted by the songs of fools[6]

▼ "Is there in the whole world one person so restrained by modesty that he or she needs no reproof, like a horse so excellently trained that it needs no whip?" (Dhammapada 10:15)

7 No one is ever completely free from the seductions of self and the hardening of heart that accompanies it. Those who seek to walk the way of *hevel*, the way of self-emptying, are wise to walk with a companion who welcomes and provides correction whenever needed. This is the kind of friendship Koheleth urges you to cultivate, and the kind of friend you should strive to be.

8 Quick anger arises from fear; you hear something that threatens your ideas and ideals. Rather than cultivate the patience to see why you feel threatened, you lash out to protect your opinions. A nursed anger arises from jealousy. You imagine another has escaped *hevel* and found permanence, and you resent that person for it. Rather than cultivate the patience to see that there is no escape from *hevel*, you burn with envy and drive out all compassion for self and others.

9 There is no escape from *hevel*—impermanence, insecurity, not knowing. Nostalgia for a past without *hevel*, a past that never was, is foolish. The past is past because the present is *hevel*, endless emptying. Forget about the past and abandon fantasies about the future, and deal wisely with the fleeting moment at hand.

10 You may not have the capacity to devote your life to wisdom, to peer into the truth of *hevel*, and to discover for yourself how to live well in a world without certainty and permanence, but you can support and learn from those who do.

7:6
whose laughter, though loud,
is but the meaningless popping of hot thorns;

7:7
their mocking can seduce
even the wise to foolishness;
posing as gifts,
they rob you of compassion.[7]

7:8
How a things ends
is more valuable than how it begins;
hence patience is more valuable than pride.

7:9
Do not be quick to anger
nor nurse anger in your heart.[8]

7:10
Don't distract yourself
with fantasies of a golden age,
imagining yesterday was better than today.
Nothing constructive can come from such nonsense.[9]

7:11
It is good to support those devoted to wisdom,
for their efforts benefit all of us,[10]

11 Sitting in the shadow of wisdom is to benefit from the teachings of those fearless enough to face the truth of *hevel* directly. Embracing wisdom is learning to live with uncertainty, to free yourself from all but the four essentials: simple food, moderate drink, meaningful work, and loving friends.

12 Reality is greater than you. Your task isn't to create a world mirroring your every whim, but to navigate the world as it presents itself to you in each and every moment. Trying to straighten the twisted robs you of the opportunity to appreciate the beauty of curves.

13 The foolish cling to moments of joy and thus make moments of sorrow all the more painful. The wise rejoice when happy and cry when sad. Clinging to neither, they leave no moment unlived and die without regret.

14 You want a world rooted in justice, a world where the good flourish and the wicked flounder. But the world you want is not the world that is. The real world is *hevel*, with one thing emptying into the next without regard for what you want or what you imagine is just and right. The foolish rail against the world; the wise learn to live with it.

⤳ "Rabbi Yannai teaches: No one can fathom the peace of the wicked or the suffering of the just." (*Pirke Avot* 4:19)

7:12
and to sit in wisdom's shadow
is to take refuge in true wealth,
since wisdom preserves the life
of those who embrace her.[11]

7:13
Contemplate the nature of reality:
none can straighten what life makes twisted.[12]

7:14
Rejoice when things go well,
yet expect change and reversals,
for that is the way of reality—
manifesting everything and its opposite
in order that you leave nothing behind.[13]

7:15
No absurdity escapes my sight:
the righteous sometimes perish
despite their goodness,
while the wicked sometimes prosper
despite their wickedness.

7:16
Don't put your faith
in goodness or wisdom—
this only courts depression.

7:17
And don't obsess over evil or foolishness—
this only courts an early death.[14]

15 There is no avoiding either suffering or joy. Don't cling to anything, and don't flee from anything; simply engage what is when it is, and gracefully allow it to pass when it does.

⤳ "Those who are free from illusion, who have seen the infinite void, who have ceased to cling to impermanent things, who have removed temptations, and who have renounced desires—they are indeed the greatest ones of all." (Dhammapada 16:8)

16 While it is true that wisdom cannot protect you from suffering, it is also true that wisdom is the best defense against the unnecessary suffering that arises when you refuse to live life as it is.

17 Striving for perfection—striving to be only righteous or just or good—is a trap denying the very nature of reality as *havel havalim*, emptying and impermanent. Wisdom makes plain when you act well and when you act poorly, and the gift of wisdom is humility and compassion. Humility frees you from demanding perfection of yourself; compassion frees you from demanding perfection of others.

⤳ "[Ben Azzai] used to teach: Scorn no one, and mock nothing, for no one is without her hour, and no thing without its place." (*Pirke Avot* 4:3)

⤳ "There never was, there never will be, and there is not now a person blamed all the time or praised all the time." (Dhammapada 17:8)

7:18
What is best is to engage the one
without shunning the other;
for living in harmony with emptying,
you move lightly through them both.[15]

7:19
Thus wisdom defends the wise
better than walls defend the princes
who live behind them.[16]

7:20
No one on earth is so perfect
as to never make mistakes,
doing good only and never erring.

7:21
So don't obsess over everything
people say about you;
even your employees
may complain about you now and then

7:22
just as you know in your heart
you complain about them.[17]

7:23
Wisdom confirms all these truths,
yet there are still things that elude me:

18 There are dimensions of reality you cannot fathom. Mystery is part of life, and embracing mystery keeps you humble. Yet there is much that can be known, and this you must examine for yourself, beginning with yourself.

➤ "Let wise ones monitor the mind, which is subtle, difficult to perceive, and restless. A mind well monitored brings happiness." (Dhammapada 3:3)

➤ "The unity is said to be the mystery. Mystery of mysteries, the door to all wonders." (Tao te Ching 1)

19 In patriarchal societies where women have little and where their status is linked to that of their fathers, husbands, or sons, Koheleth sees an evil peculiar to women: wasting your life trying to snare a man. No one can secure your future, for the future is by nature insecure. Women no less than men are urged to relinquish all efforts aimed at security and embrace the path of the wise: eat simply, drink moderately, work constructively, and love deeply.

20 The only men ensnared this way are those foolish enough to believe that they can provide security, wealth, power, and prestige. The wise, both women and men, abandon the mad quest for security and cultivate love and friendship only among those at peace with *hevel*.

7:24
The essence of existence,
the deep of the deep—
who can find that?

7:25
I accept my limits
and focus mind and heart
on what can be known;[18]
probing wisely and investigating rationally
the evil of folly and the madness of fools.

7:26
What I found was more bitter than death:
women who have turned themselves into snares,
their hearts into nets,
and their arms into chains.[19]
But the wise escape,
and only the foolish are caught.[20]

21 Even after all your investigations, do not imagine a definitive answer to life has been found. Why? Because life isn't a question to be answered, but a mystery to be lived.

22 And don't imagine that the opposite sex is the problem or that you need to become an ascetic and avoid all relationships. Even among celibate seekers of truth Koheleth finds only one in a thousand who has insight into reality.

~ "Among thousands of people, scarcely one strives for perfection." (Bhagavad Gita 7:3)

~ "Few among all people reach the other shore. The others merely run up and down this shore." (Dhammapada 6:10)

~ "Jesus said: I will choose one of you out of a thousand and two of you out of ten thousand. They will stand up and they will be alone." (Gospel of Thomas, Logiaon 23)

23 Male or female, the truth is the same: If you want to find joy in life, live simply: eat simply, drink moderately, work constructively, and cultivate a few close friends. That's it. But chances are you can't accept that. You want something more complicated. You want something you have to spend your life pursuing, something so rare that when you die without it you do not despair but imagine it was just too rare to find. Nonsense. Life is simple; joy is simple; but only if you have the courage to live simply enough to experience it.

7:27
Look: after all I have discovered,
after piling one thing upon another
to reach a conclusion—

7:28
the conclusion still eludes me![21]
Even among a thousand men
without a woman among them,
only one may be wise.[22]

7:29
What I did find was this:
reality is simple,
but we insist on complicating it.[23]

1 Living from folly is exhausting and leaves you troubled and anxious. Your breathing is vexed, and your face bears the scars of stress. Wisdom transforms all this, and the mark of the wise is a tranquil and untroubled face.

2 Being wise does not exempt you from the whim of the powerful. When you cannot avoid their demands, do what is asked of you swiftly, and in this way return to living simply all the more quickly.

3 While you may not be able to avoid the powerful, don't be intimidated by them. They, no less than you, are subject to *hevel*: the wild uncertainty of life, and the stark inevitability of death. So show them deference if you must, but not fear. Do what is necessary, disengage from them when you can, and deny them the pleasure of seeing you sweat.

4 There is no point in directly challenging the foolishness of the powerful. Better to seek wisdom and let their own foolishness consume them.

☐ Chapter Eight

8:1
Who compares to the wise?
Who else knows the meaning of things?
Wisdom brightens your face
and softens your features.[1]

8:2
Yet even I take seriously
the demands of the powerful,
fulfilling them as if
I were fulfilling a sacred vow.[2]

8:3
But show no fear before the powerful,
and disengage from them calmly.
Do your best to avoid
collaborating with their evil,
but know that they can do
whatever they please.[3]

8:4
Their word becomes law,
and none dare say, "What are you doing?"[4]

5   The powerful are drunk on power and the fantasy that power equates to permanence. Unlike the wise, they do not watch the shifting of moments and are surprised and panicked when power slips from their grasp. This reversal of fortune could be a catalyst for wisdom, but for those addicted to power it is only a descent into hell.

6   Death is the great leveler: rich and poor, powerful and powerless, wise and foolish all die and share the same fate. For the rich, powerful, and foolish, the advent of death is a horror, stripping away their illusion of permanence. For the wise, it is but the next moment to be welcomed as all moments are welcomed—with an open heart and tranquil mind.

⟿   "Sages look equally upon all, whether it be a minister of learning and humanity or an infidel, or whether it be a cow, an elephant, or a dog." (Bhagavad Gita 5:18)

8:5
You will not be blamed
if coerced to comply,
for the wise know that justice, too, has its time.

8:6
Indeed everything has its time and its retribution,
and the wicked will topple from their own evil.[5]

8:7
They cannot imagine this happening,
and even as the end approaches,
they will not heed those who warn them.

8:8
You cannot escape
the consequence of your actions
or hold back the inevitable;
even the most powerful
lack authority over death;
no weapons can war against it;
and no amount of evil can save them.[6]

8:9
All this I perceived,
and I set my heart to fathom
every action under heaven,
and I saw that while there are those who oppress others,
in the end the evil they create cannot save them.

7 Society honors the powerful, even if they are scoundrels and thieves, even if their policies cause massive loss of life and livelihood. Fame falls to those who make spectacles of themselves or who place themselves at the heart of others' spectacles. The wise avoid all of this, seeking neither fame nor fortune. The wise know that joy is found not in power, but in simplicity; not in being front and center, but in being low and hidden. This is why they go unremembered.

8 It is easy to believe that the evil triumph, but the wise know better. No one triumphs; no one wins. There is no winning or losing in a world of impermanence and change. So is there any advantage to wisdom over wickedness? Yes, for the wise know the way of *hevel*, the way of continual emptying, and this allows them to find true joy, while the wicked place their faith in power, only to have it taken from them by those more powerful still.

~ "Receive wealth or prosperity without arrogance; and be ready to let it go." (Meditations of Marcus Aurelius 8:33)

~ "A good man brings good things out of his storehouse, but a bad man brings bad things from his storehouse (which is in his heart). And he says bad things. For out of the surplus in his heart he brings out bad things." (Gospel of Thomas, logiaon 45b)

8:10
And yet I saw as well that even in death
the wicked are honored with pomp and ceremony,
and a new generation of evil arises to take their place.
And the righteous who sought to do good?
The city forgets them. How absurd![7]

8:11
It is because justice is delayed that evil persists;

8:12
and because we see the wicked living long lives,
we doubt the godly will prevail.
But I do not doubt,

8:13
and the wicked will fade like shadows,
for they do not honor the way of reality.[8]

8:14
Here is another absurdity rampant on earth:
the righteous are treated as sinners,
while the sinners are hailed as righteous.
This is madness!

8:15
This is why I value joy,
for there is nothing better
for you to do during your life
than to eat, drink, and rejoice.
This purpose should inform all your labor
throughout your life under the sun.

9 Not knowing is the key to living with *hevel*, perpetual emptying and impermanence. All knowing is contingent on the moment, and no more lasting than that. When you give up the pretense of knowing and accept the reality of not knowing, you find yourself at peace with life.

⌐ "To know that you do not know is highest. To not know but think you know is flawed." (Tao te Ching 71)

8:16
This I concluded
after ceaselessly turning my heart to wisdom
and observing all that is done on this earth.

8:17
I looked into every aspect of reality
and still could not fathom
all that happens under the sun.
Try as you will, none can fathom it fully.
Even if you pretend to know,
in truth you do not.[9]

1 Wisdom places you in the palm of reality, that is to say, it reveals to you that all things are part of the flow of *hevel*. But do not imagine that this leads only to goodness and love, for that is not the way of reality. Love and hate are equally real, and which comes to you when is not for you to know. This is the fierce faith of Koheleth: you cannot know what is next, only that whatever it is—good or bad—it is the reality you must confront.

2 There is no escape from reality or the good and ill reality holds. The advantage wisdom offers is not the avoidance of suffering, but knowing how to suffer not one moment longer than necessary.

☐ Chapter Nine

9:1

I sifted through all of this
and found that both
the righteous and the wise
rest in the palm of reality,
and whether this leads to love or hate,
none can know,
for every possibility lies before you.[1]

9:2

All things come to all people;
the good are not privileged,
and no distinction is made between
the pure and the impure,
or the pious and the impious.
In this there is no advantage
to being saint or sinner,
rash or cautious.[2]

3 Where wisdom teaches you how to minimize suffering, foolishness causes you to wallow in it.

4 Trusting life, you engage and release both joy and suffering, knowing that all things come and all things pass away. This knowing opens your heart to compassion for all the living.

5 While a dog may be despised and a lion feared, the wise are not bothered by such distinctions. The only distinction that matters to them is living or dead, and they prefer the former to the latter, all the while knowing that both are inevitable.

6 As long as you have life you can contemplate the fact of your death, and this will free you to live simply and well.

~ "All conditioned things are involved in suffering. The one who knows and perceives this fact ceases to be miserable. This is the way to purity of vision." (Dhammapada 20:6)

7 Reality doesn't prefer one thing to another, though from your point of view preference is inevitable.

~ "Heaven and earth are impartial and regard myriad things as straw dogs. The sages are impartial and regard people as straw dogs." (Tao te Ching 5)

9:3
There is a relentlessness
to all that happens under the sun,
and the same fate awaits us all.
This fills the small-hearted with fear,
and drives the small-minded mad,
and their lives are so marked
until they die.[3]

9:4
But one devoted to life
trusts life;[4]
better to be a live dog
than a dead lion.[5]

9:5
For the living can know
that death awaits them,
while the dead know nothing at all
and lack any reward.
And soon all memory of them
will be forgotten.[6]

9:6
Their loves, their hates,
their passions perish with them,
and they no longer matter to the world.[7]

8 White garments are simple garments—neither dyed nor adorned. Anointing your head with oil gives you some relief from the heat. Koheleth is in effect saying: dress simply and avoid getting overheated by either the sun or your opinions.

~ "Adorn yourself with simplicity and modesty and with indifference toward the things that lie between virtue and vice." (Meditations of Marcus Aurelius 7:31)

~ "Jesus said: Do not worry from morning to evening or evening to morning about what you are going to wear." (Gospel of Thomas, logiaon 36)

~ "Modesty and faith are two that go together. If one is removed, the other is also removed." (Prophet Muhammad, in Sultan, *The Qur'an and Sayings of Prophet Muhammad*, p. 121)

9 Love, although as impermanent as everything else, is key to living well and wisely.

10 You are the way reality mows your lawn, picks up after your dog, and cures cancer. Nothing more and nothing less. Joy comes from being responsive to life's call to action, whatever that action may be.

9:7
So here is my guidance
and the right path:
eat your bread with joy,
and drink your wine with gladness;

9:8
let your clothes be white,
and let your head never lack for oil;[8]

9:9
find a beloved with whom
to share your life—
no matter how long or short.
This is what makes your life
and your labor worthwhile.[9]

9:10
Whatever falls into your hand to do,
do it without hesitation.
For in the grave
there is neither doing, nor reason,
nor knowledge, nor wisdom.[10]

11 There is but one guarantee in life, and that is death. Nothing else is promised you: the swift can lose a race, and the mighty can fall in battle; the worldly and clever can still go hungry, and the scholar can toil in obscurity. But you shouldn't care about any of this because there is nothing you can do about it. You are not trying to escape the reality of life, but to navigate it with a modicum of joy and tranquility. And this requires that you don't cling to outcomes but find meaning in action alone. If you do all you can in this moment, there is nothing more you can do than step back and await the call of the next moment. In this alone there is satisfaction.

⤳ "You have only the right to work, but none to the fruit thereof. Let not then the fruit of your action be your motive, nor yet be enamored of inaction." (Bhagavad Gita 2:47)

12 But do not imagine that doing all you can in this moment prevents you from dying in the next. Knowing that death is inevitable and that its timing is unknowable, you are free to engage this moment without fear, and when fear is gone, joy is present.

⤳ "The one who meddles will fail; the one who grasps will lose. Therefore, sages do not meddle and thus do not fail. They do not grasp and thus do not lose." (Tao te Ching 64)

9:11
Another observation
about this world:
the swiftest runner
does not always win the race,
nor the does the battle
always go to the strong;
even the wise can go hungry,
and the clever can be poor;
and the scholar can live without acclaim.
Only mortality and death happen to us all.[11]

9:12
You cannot know how you will die;
death befalls you without warning,
as the net traps the fish
and the snare downs the bird.[12]

9:13
There is yet something else
that pains me deeply:

9:14
There was once a small
and undefended town,
sparsely populated.
A mighty king besieged it,
surrounding it with towering battlements.

13 If you seek wisdom in order to gain fame, your search is in vain. The sage does what is right because it is right, and leaves thoughts of reward and remembrance to the foolish.

14 While it is true that wisdom guarantees nothing, it is still superior to folly, for it holds out the promise of peace even if it cannot guarantee peace. But beware the false sage, the charlatan who captures minds and hearts by making claims and promises rooted in delusion and deceit. Once the people lose faith in the wise, it is only a matter of time before they lose faith in wisdom as well.

9:15
Having taken the town,
the king was intent on slaughtering the people,
but a penniless sage confronted him
and negotiated the salvation of the people.
Did the people remember and applaud this sage?
Of course not![13]

9:16
Still, wisdom is superior to warfare,
even if the wise are impoverished,
derided, and ignored;

9:17
for soft words from the wise
can trump the war cry of kings
and the shrieking rants of fools;

9:18
wisdom is preferable to weapons,
though a false sage can undo much good.[14]

[1] Fools complicate the simple and chase after wind. They are always shocked and caught off guard by the natural turning of events. No matter how loudly people may lay claim to wisdom, if they stumble where there is nothing to stumble over, you can be certain their claims are false.

[~] "Walkers of the way who delight in vigilance, fearing thoughtlessness, move like fire, burning away all obstacles large and small." (Dhammapada 2:11)

[~] "Walkers of the way who delight in vigilance, fearing thoughtlessness, cannot fall back—they are close to freedom already." (Dhammapada 2:12)

[2] Do not resist the powerful with brute force. Do not pit your will against their will. Rather observe the direction they are rushing and offer no resistance, but add your will to theirs that they may topple of their own accord. The supple tree bends with the wind; the stout one is broken by it.

[~] "Thus that which is hard and stiff is the follower of death; that which is soft and yielding is the follower of life." (Tao te Ching 76)

[~] "Nothing in the world is softer or weaker than water, yet nothing is better at overcoming the hard and strong." (Tao te Ching 78)

☐ Chapter Ten

10:1
Just as a dead fly
sours a perfumer's oil,
so even a little stupidity
undermines wisdom
and unravels a fine reputation.

10:2
The wise heart
inclines toward what is right
while the foolish heart leans into folly.

10:3
The foolish stumble
even on a paved road;
this is how you know them to be fools.[1]

10:4
If the powerful blow against you,
hold your place, but do not resist;
defeat them through yielding.[2]

3 Danger and reversal are everywhere. There is no safety; there is no security. Learn to live with radical uncertainty.

4 Even everyday tasks can turn disastrous. There is no avoiding the reversal of events; that is the nature of *hevel*.

5 Avoiding little tasks only turns them into bigger ones.

10:5
See what I have seen:
that the madness of this world
is so deeply ingrained
that it might as well be law;

10:6
that fools rise to power,
and the once wealthy dwell in slums;

10:7
that former slaves ride fine horses,
and former financiers walk barefoot like slaves.[3]

10:8
If you dig a pit,
you will fall into it;
and if you smash a wall,
the snake dwelling within its rocks
will bite you;

10:9
quarrymen are crushed by rock;
and lumberjacks are felled by logs.[4]

10:10
A dull ax left unsharpened
makes chopping all the more arduous.
Wisdom tells you this.[5]

6 Wisdom unapplied is useless.

7 Those who seek to pass themselves off as wise often bury their foolishness in convoluted talk. Do not be taken in by well-crafted sentences
or well-delivered speeches. Do not imagine that a large audience
implies a wise message. The good life is simple—eat and drink in moderation, engage in meaningful work, avoid loneliness by cultivating
good friends—but people complicate things in order to avoid having to
face the reality of life and do the work of right living.

8 Koheleth is talking about leaders hungry for power and money who
fear the future and so gobble up all they can in the present. Their concern
is only for themselves, and their actions undermine the lives of others.

～ "Fools with little understanding are their own greatest enemies, for
they do evil deeds which must bear bitter fruits." (Dhammapada 5:7)

9 I have moved verse 17 to follow verse 20, allowing Koheleth's four
anti-foolish-leader verses (16, 18, 19, 20) to appear as a whole.

10:11
A snake charmer who delays in charming will be bit.[6]

10:12
The words of the wise are self-effacing;
those of the fool are self-destructive;

10:13
Fools begin arguments with foolishness
and lead inexorably to insanity and evil.

10:14
They pile words upon words,
masking ignorance with prophetic babbling,
but none can know what the future holds.

10:15
The labor of fools is exhausting
and brings them no closer to their destination.[7]

10:16
The earth is doomed
when dominated by adolescent leaders,
child-princes who devour all from the beginning.[8, 9]

10 Foolish leaders are driven by immediate gratification. They feel no compunction allowing the world to go to ruin as long as they themselves do not suffer. What money they have they use for themselves and do nothing to alleviate misery.

11 Foolish leaders lead through fear and intimidation, forcing neighbor to spy on neighbor, and children to spy on parents. Theirs is a world stripped of trust.

12 The wise lead by example: acting in harmony with life for the benefit of the living.

➤ "Those who are free from illusion, who have seen the infinite void, who have ceased to cling to impermanent things, who have removed temptations, and who have renounced desires—they are indeed the greatest ones of all." (Dhammapada 7:8)

10:18
Refusing to lift a finger
or spend a dollar,
they allow roofs to sag
and houses to leak;

10:19
spending lavishly on bread
and drunken spectacle,
their wealth explains the earth's affliction.[10]

10:20
Yet don't even fantasize about revolution,
or curse the rich
even in the privacy of your bedroom,
for spies circle overhead like parrots,
repeating your words and betraying you.[11]

10:17
But blessed is a world led by the wise
who master their appetites
and consume in harmony with nature.[12]

1 Koheleth is referring to philanthropy. Casting your generosity widely allows it to flow where it is most needed, for just as water seeks the lowest point, so generosity finds its way to those with the least.

➤ "The highest goodness resembles water. Water greatly benefits myriad things without contention. It stays in places that people dislike. Therefore it is similar to the Tao." (Tao te Ching 8)

➤ "The stingy do not go to the world of the gods. Fools only do not praise generosity. A wise one rejoices in generosity and through it becomes blessed in the other world." (Dhammapada 13:11)

➤ "The best charity is to feed an empty stomach." (Prophet Muhammad, in Sultan, *The Qur'an and Sayings of Prophet Muhammad*, p. 133)

2 Being generous to others will encourage others to be generous to you.

➤ "Sages do not accumulate. The more they assist others, the more they possess; the more they give to others, the more they gain." (Tao te Ching 81)

3 Do not simply give to the crisis at hand, but broaden your area of concern so that you can be of help to those to whom the worst has not yet happened.

4 The realities of life are unavoidable: rain clouds spill rain; fallen trees do not right themselves. In other words, things happen when the conditions for them to happen are ripe. What is done must be done and cannot be undone. Yet …

5 If you wait for ideal conditions before taking action, you may never take action, for you cannot know which moment is the perfect moment. All you know is the moment at hand. Do what you can with reality as it is, and do not let the quest for perfection excuse inaction.

☐ Chapter Eleven

11:1
Toss your bread upon the waters,[1]
and in time you will find it again.[2]

11:2
Give widely to seven or even eight,
for you cannot know
where tragedy will fall on the earth.[3]

11:3
Clouds heavy with rain
will drench the earth;
a fallen tree remains fallen,
be it in the north or the south.[4]

11:4
Those who watch the wind will never sow,
and those who watch the clouds will never reap.[5]

6 Just as there is no perfect moment, there is no perfect knowing, no certainty. To remain inactive until you are certain of the result is to do nothing at all. So accept uncertainty, and do what you can when you can.

7 While you cannot be certain that your planting will yield a good harvest, you can be sure that not planting will yield no harvest at all. So act without knowing the result. Live your life as an experiment, and take comfort in curiosity rather than certainty.

~ "For nobody lights a lamp and puts it underneath a bushel basket or in a hidden place. Rather, it is placed on a lamp stand so that all who go in and out may see the light." (Gospel of Thomas, logiaon 33b)

8 *Hevel*, the ceaseless emptying of life and the uncertainty it generates, is no cause for despair. There is morning—enjoy it! There is evening—enjoy that as well. While there may be nothing new under the sun, still each moment is fresh. Only the curious live without fear, taking pleasure in each day's unfolding.

9 Yet do not cling to light or freshness, for dark days—days of suffering, loss, and depression—too will be many. There is no escaping the rising and falling of things, the coming and going of moments. Enjoy what there is while it is, and let it pass when the time to pass comes due.

10 Wisdom should not make you old before your time. Knowing that everything is in the process of emptying—that nothing is permanent, certain, and secure—should not leave you paralyzed. On the contrary, live always in sync with the moment: when the young give in to the madness of youth, just don't go so far as to do things that cause needless pain and suffering.

11 Sometimes being called to account is obvious: the way an alcoholic suffers from liver disease or a lifelong smoker dies of lung cancer. Sometimes it is more subtle, so subtle that none can fathom it, though in the recesses of your heart you may suspect that your foolishness has robbed you of joys unimaginable.

11:5
Just as none can know
the way of the wind,
nor predict the life
of one as yet unborn,
so you cannot fathom the way of reality.[6]

11:6
Nevertheless, plant seed in the morning,
and do not let your hands be idle in the evening.
There is no way to know
which of your efforts
—this one or that one—
will succeed,
and perhaps both may turn out for the good![7]

11:7
Light is sweet,
and it is good that the eyes see the sun,

11:8
so cherish each day
no matter how many you have;[8]
and yet know that days of darkness, too, will be many.
For all that arises is fated to fall.[9]

11:9
Let the young rejoice in their youth
and follow their heart's desires,
pursuing all that the eye sees;[10]
but know that every choice has its consequence,
and reality will call you to account.[11]

12 Yet do not despair over past choices or the consequences they set in motion. There is nothing you can do to avoid the moments to come. So don't worry about the next moment, and seek only to engage this moment wisely and well. Don't deny the body or despise it; it will turn on itself soon enough. While you are healthy, act boldly; while you are strong, act fearlessly. There will be time enough for hesitation and dread when health and strength are gone.

"The one who knows that this body is like froth, as unsubstantial as a mirage, will break the flower-tipped arrow of Mara [attachment to permanence] and never see the king of death." (Dhammapada 4:3)

11:10
Banish worry from your heart,
and do not mortify your flesh,
for the brightness of youth
and the darkness of age
are both empty and impermanent.[12]

1 What is your origin? Where did you come from? From *hevel*; from the ceaseless rising and falling of reality. To realize your beginning is to realize your end. And to know them both is to be free from worrying about either.

~ "Jesus said: Blessed are the single ones [those who have seen the unity at the heart of all diversity] and the chosen ones, for you will find the Kingdom. Because you emerged from it, you will return to it." (Gospel of Thomas, logiaon 48)

2 The next seven verses offer a metaphoric examination of old age. The following notes simply make Koheleth's metaphors plain.

3 Your eyes grow cloudy with cataracts.

4 The house guards are your limbs, and the warriors are your back.

~ "This body is a painted image, covered with wounds, bunched together, sickly, and impermanent." (Dhammapada 11:2)

5 Your teeth.

6 Your eyes.

7 You cannot move your bowels.

8 Your digestion is poor.

9 You cannot sleep through the night for all the noise, yet you cannot hear people speaking to you during the day.

☐ Chapter Twelve

12:1
Yet even in your youth
remember your origin,[1]
and do not wait for tragedy and old age
to realize the emptiness of pleasure.[2]

12:2
But seek the truth
before the sun, light,
moon, and stars grow dim,
and clouds return following a rain;[3]

12:3
before the house guards tremble,
and warriors stoop;[4]
before the grinding maids[5]
grow few and idle,
and the watchers at the windows grow dim;[6]

12:4
before the doors to the street are bolted,[7]
and the sound of grinding is low;[8]
before your sleep is broken by a chirping bird,
and yet a choir's voice sounds muffled;[9]

10 Your balance is wobbly, and you fear stumbling over any uneven surface.

11 Your nerves are so sensitive that almost anything causes irritation.

12 Your spinal column loses all flexibility, and your back is in spasm.

13 You fall and crack your skull.

14 You suffer from vomiting and acid reflux.

15 You become incontinent.

16 Before you suffer the difficulties of old age, realize the true nature of reality as *hevel*. Knowing that everything passes away allows you to accept the fading of youth and helps you prepare for the limitations and indignities of old age. Knowing that these too are impermanent will allow you to experience them without excess fear or anxiety. Old age is no more permanent than youth.

> "Knowing that one's body is fragile like a clay pot, and making one's mind firm like a fortress, one should attack Mara [attachment to permanence] with the weapon of wisdom." (Dhammapada 3:8)

17 Just as your life ends as it began, from dust to dust, so Ecclesiastes ends as it began, with an affirmation of the inescapable truth of reality: *havel havalim*, everything is *hevel*, everything is as fleeting and as insubstantial as breath.

18 Chapter 12 doesn't end with verse 8 and in fact continues for six more verses. I have chosen to separate these verses from the rest of the chapter for two reasons. First, there is a consensus among scholars that the remaining verses were added to the original text at a later date in order to make Ecclesiastes conform to more mainstream Jewish notions of God and God's commandments. Second, the last verses are no longer the words of Koheleth but words about him.

12:5

before you fear even a slight incline,
and travel becomes terrifying;[10]
before even an almond blossom
or resting grasshopper
weighs too heavy on you;[11]
before all desire fades;
before your friends die,
and the streets fill with mourners;

12:6

before the silver cord snaps,[12]
and the golden bowl cracks;[13]
before the pitcher breaks at the spring,[14]
and the bucket shatters at the well.[15]

12:7

Before all this, know that
dust returns to the earth as it was,
and breath returns to the source that breathed it.[16]

12:8

Emptiness upon emptiness
—said the Assembler—
everything is a passing away.[17, 18]

1 The reference here is to the biblical Book of Proverbs, which, like Ecclesiastes, is traditionally though erroneously ascribed to King Solomon.

2 The wisdom of Koheleth is valuable only if you to live by them, only if you liberate yourself from folly and shape your life by what is good: eating simply, drinking moderately, working constructively, and loving deeply.

~ "By one's self the evil is done; by one's self one suffers. By one's self evil is left undone; by one's self one is purified." (Dhammapada 12:9)

3 Just as nails well placed hold things together, so wisdom well placed holds meaning and purpose together.

4 The one Shepherd is not god in any anthropomorphic sense, but The God, reality itself. Koheleth is the Assembler of Wisdom, not its creator. Ecclesiastes is a book of reasoned insight, not revealed truth. Koheleth did what you can do: examine the nature of reality and see what is true. Not true for him or true for you or true for some elect or elite, but true for all.

If nothing else, let this book be a catalyst to your own investigations. Look for yourself and see what is so, and live in harmony with reality, for to do anything less is needless vexing of heart, mind, and spirit, robbing you of the only joy there is: living in harmony with the moment, no matter what it contains.

5 The compilations of the wise are worthy of study, but do not imagine that they are the only books being published. Every author lays claim to wisdom, but few actually have it. Do not put your faith in any book, but only in those whose wisdom you can attest.

6 Just as there is no end to the making of books, so is there no end to the study of them. But wisdom is not complicated, and Koheleth sought to write plainly. If you have to exhaust yourself making sense of another's wisdom, chances are it isn't all that wise.

☐ Epilogue
(Chapter Twelve, Continued)

12:9
The Assembler was a sage;
he not only investigated truth,
he taught it to the people as well.
He listened closely
and examined the world's wisdom
and compiled many proverbs.[1]

12:10
The Assembler sought out truth
and expounded it plainly.

12:11
The words of the wise prod;[2]
and the anthologies of the sages
are well-hammered nails[3]
and all come from one Shepherd.[4]

12:12
Beyond these, my friends, beware,
for there is no end to the compiling of books,[5]
and endless examination exhausts the flesh.[6]

7 Here is the literal translation of the final two verses of Ecclesiastes: "The end of the matter when all is done: Fear The God and observe His commandments! For this applies to all humankind: that The God will judge every deed good or ill, even those that are hidden." Despite the editor's continued use of "The God," *HaElohim*, he is clearly referring to the anthropomorphic God of the Jews and the commandments found in Torah. This is the attempt of a later editor to bring the radical wisdom of Koheleth into line with the conventional wisdom and theology of mainstream Judaism.

My own rendering attempts to read these added verses in light of Koheleth's original text. The God is reality, and the universal imperative of the wise is to eat simply, drink moderately, work meaningfully, and cultivate love and friendship.

8 What is good? Living with wisdom and thus eating wisely, drinking moderately, working meaningfully, and cultivating love and friendship. What is evil? Living foolishly, and pursuing power, fame, wealth, and permanence.

~ "As a solid rock is not moved by the wind, wise people are not shaken by blame or by praise." (Dhammapada 6:6)

12:13
After all has been heard,
the end of the matter is this:
Regarding reality—wonder!
Regarding right living—diligence!
This is true for everyone,[7]

12:14
for reality responds to every deed,
hidden and known, good or bad,
and yields its judgment.[8]

Bibliography

Antinoff, Steve. *Spiritual Atheism*. Berkeley: Counterpoint, 2009.

Bergant, Dianne. *What Are They Saying about Wisdom Literature?* New York: Paulist Press, 1984.

Bloom, Harold. *Where Shall Wisdom Be Found?* New York: Riverhead Books, 2004.

Brenner, Athalya, ed. *A Feminist Companion to Wisdom Literature*. Sheffield, UK: Sheffield Academic Press, 1995.

Brueggemann, Walter. *In Man We Trust: The Neglected Side of Biblical Faith*. Richmond, VA: John Knox Press, 1972.

Bryce, Glendon E. *A Legacy of Wisdom: The Egyptian Contribution to the Wisdom of Israel*. Lewisburg, PA: Bucknell University Press, 1979.

Burroughs, Kendra. *Bhagavad Gita: Annotated & Explained*. Translated by Shri Swami Purohit. Woodstock, VT: SkyLight Paths, 2002.

Charlesworth, James, and Michael Daise, eds. *Light in a Spotless Mirror: Reflections on Wisdom Traditions in Judaism and Early Christianity*. Harrisburg, PA: Trinity Press International, 2003.

Christianson, Eric. *Ecclesiastes Through the Centuries*. Malden, MA: Blackwell Publishing, 2007.

Collins, John J. *Jewish Wisdom in the Hellenistic Age*. Louisville: Westminster John Knox Press, 1997.

Crenshaw, James L. *Ecclesiastes*. Richmond VA: John Knox Press, 1987.

———. *Old Testament Wisdom: An Introduction*. 3rd ed. Atlanta: John Knox Press, 2010.

Davies, Stevan. *The Gospel of Thomas: Annotated & Explained*. Woodstock, VT: SkyLight Paths, 2004.

Dillon, Emile Joseph. *The Skeptics of the Old Testament*. New York: Haskell House Publishers, 1973.

Fox, Michael, V. *Ecclesiastes*. The JPS Bible Commentary. Philadelphia: Jewish Publication Society, 2004.

———. *A Time to Tear Down and a Time to Build Up: A Rereading of Ecclesiastes*. Grand Rapids, MI: Wm. B. Eerdmans Publishing, 1999.

Fredericks, Daniel C. *Coping with Transience: Ecclesiastes on Brevity in Life*. Sheffield, UK: JSOT Press, 1993.

Gammie, John G., and Leo G. Perdue, eds. *The Sage in Israel and the Ancient Near East*. Winona Lake, IN: Eisenbrauns, 1990.

Gordis, Robert. *The Wisdom of Ecclesiastes*. New York: Berhman House, 1945.

Knobel, Peter S. *The Targum of Qohelet*. The Aramaic Bible, vol. 15. Collegeville, MN: Liturgical Press, 1991.

Kushner, Harold. *When All You've Ever Wanted Isn't Enough*. New York: Fireside, 1986.

Leithart, Peter. *Solomon Among the Postmoderns*. Grand Rapids, MI: Brazos Press, 2008.

Limburg, James. *Encountering Ecclesiastes: A Book for Our Time*. Grand Rapids, MI: W. B. Eerdmans Publishing, 2006.

Lin, Derek. *Tao Te Ching: Annotated & Explained*. Woodstock, VT: SkyLight Paths, 2009.

Lohfink, Norbert. *Qoheleth: A Continental Commentary*. Minneapolis: Augsburg Fortress Publishers, 2002.

Mack, Burton. *Wisdom and the Hebrew Epic. Ben Sira's Hymn in Praise of the Fathers*. Chicago: University of Chicago Press, 1985.

Maguire, Jack. *Dhammapada: Annotated & Explained*. Translated by Max Müller. Woodstock, VT: SkyLight Paths, 2002.

McKane, William. *Prophets and Wise Men*. Philadelphia: Wipf & Stock Publishers, 2005.

McNeil, Russell. *The Meditations of Marcus Aurelius: Selections Annotated & Explained*. Translated by George Long. Woodstock, VT: SkyLight Paths, 2007.

Meyers, Jeffery. *Ecclesiastes Through New Eyes*. Monroe, LA: Athanasius Press, 2007.

Mitchell, Stephen. *The Book of Job*. New York: Harper Perennial, 1992.

Morgan, Donn. *Wisdom in the Old Testament Traditions*. Atlanta: John Knox, 1981.

Murphy, Roland E. *Ecclesiastes*. Word Biblical Commentary, vol. 23. Nashville: Thomas Nelson Publishers, 1992.

———. *The Tree of Life: An Exploration of Biblical Wisdom Literature*. The Anchor Bible Reference Library. New York: Doubleday, 1990.

Nelson, Tommy. *A Life Well Lived: A Study of the Book of Ecclesiastes*. Nashville: Broadman & Holman Publishers, 2005.

O'Connor, Kathleen M. *The Wisdom Literature*. Wilmington, DE: Michael Glazier Books, 1993.

Ostriker, Alicia Suskin. *For the Love of God: The Bible as an Open Book*. New Brunswick, NJ: Rutgers University Press, 2007.

Perdue, Leo G. *The Sword and the Stylus: An Introduction to Wisdom in the Age of Empires*. Grand Rapids MI: W.B. Eerdmans Publishing, 2008.

———. *Wisdom & Creation*. Nashville: Abingdon Press, 1994.

———. *Wisdom Literature: A Theological History*. Louisville: Westminster John Knox Press, 2007.

Perry, Theodore A. *Dialogues with Kohelet*. Philadelphia: Pennsylvania State University Press, 1993.

Polish, Daniel F. "Shedding an Eastern Light on Kohelet." *CCAR Journal: The Reform Jewish Quarterly*, Fall 2009, pp. 103–22.

Schroer, Silvia. *Wisdom Has Built Her House: Studies on the Figure of Sophia in the Bible*. Translated by Linda M. Mahoney and William McDonough. Collegeville, MN: Liturgical Press, 2000.

Scott, R. B. Y. *The Way of Wisdom in the Old Testament*. New York: Macmillan, 1971.

Seow, C. L. *Ecclesiastes: A New Translation with Introduction and Commentary*. The Anchor Bible. New York: Doubleday, 1997.

Shapiro, Rami. *The Divine Feminine in Biblical Wisdom Literature: Selections Annotated & Explained*. Woodstock, VT: SkyLight Paths, 2005.

————. *Embracing the Divine Feminine: Finding God through the Ecstasy of Physical Love—The Song of Songs Annotated & Explained*. Woodstock, VT: SkyLight Paths, 2014.

————. *Ethics of the Sages: Pirke Avot—Annotated & Explained*. Woodstock, VT: SkyLight Paths, 2006.

————. *The Golden Rule and the Games People Play: The Ultimate Strategy for a Meaning-Filled Life*. Woodstock, VT: SkyLight Paths, 2015.

————. *Hasidic Tales: Annotated & Explained*. Woodstock, VT: SkyLight Paths, 2004.

————. *The Hebrew Prophets: Annotated & Explained*. Woodstock, VT: SkyLight Paths, 2004.

————. *Perennial Wisdom for the Spiritually Independent: Sacred Teachings—Annotated & Explained*. Woodstock, VT: SkyLight Paths, 2013.

————. *Recovery—The Sacred Art: The Twelve Steps as Spiritual Practice*. Woodstock, VT: SkyLight Paths, 2009.

————. *The Sacred Art of Lovingkindnesss: Preparing to Practice*. Woodstock, VT: SkyLight Paths, 2006.

————. *Tanya, the Masterpiece of Hasidic Wisdom: Annotated & Explained*. Woodstock, VT: SkyLight Paths, 2010.

————. *The Way of Solomon*. San Francisco: HarperSanFrancisco, 2000.

————. *The Wisdom of Solomon*. New York: Bell Tower, 2002.

Sultan, Sohaib. *The Qur'an and Sayings of Prophet Muhammad: Annotated & Explained*. Translated by Yusuf Ali. Woodstock, VT: SkyLight Paths, 2007.

Von Rad, Gerhard. *Wisdom in Israel*. Nashville: Abingdon, 1972.

Waddle, Ray. *Against the Grain: Unconventional Wisdom from Ecclesiastes*. Nashville: Upper Room, 2005.

Westermann, Claus. *Roots of Wisdom: The Oldest Proverbs of Israel and Other Peoples*. Louisville: Westminster John Knox Press, 1995.

Whybray, R. N. *The Intellectual Tradition in the Old Testament*. Berlin: Walter de Gruyter, 1974.

Zimmermann, Frank. *The Inner World of Qohelet*. New York: Ktav Publishing House, 1973.

Zlotowitz, Meir. *Koheles-Ecclesiastes: A New Translation with a Commentary Anthologized from Talmudic, Midrashic and Rabbinic Sources*. New York: ArtScroll, 1999.

About SKYLIGHT PATHS Publishing

SkyLight Paths Publishing is creating a place where people of different spiritual traditions come together for challenge and inspiration, a place where we can help each other understand the mystery that lies at the heart of our existence.

Through spirituality, our religious beliefs are increasingly becoming a part of our lives—rather than *apart* from our lives. While many of us may be more interested than ever in spiritual growth, we may be less firmly planted in traditional religion. Yet, we do want to deepen our relationship to the sacred, to learn from our own as well as from other faith traditions, and to practice in new ways.

SkyLight Paths sees both believers and seekers as a community that increasingly transcends traditional boundaries of religion and denomination—people wanting to learn from each other, *walking together, finding the way.*

For your information and convenience, at the back of this book we have provided a list of other SkyLight Paths books you might find interesting and useful. They cover the following subjects:

Buddhism / Zen
Catholicism
Chaplaincy
Children's Books
Christianity
Comparative
  Religion
Earth-Based
  Spirituality
Enneagram
Global Spiritual
  Perspectives

Gnosticism
Hinduism /
  Vedanta
Inspiration
Islam / Sufism
Judaism
Meditation
Mindfulness
Monasticism
Mysticism
Personal Growth

Poetry
Prayer
Religious Etiquette
Retirement & Later-
  Life Spirituality
Spiritual Biography
Spiritual Direction
Spirituality
Women's Interest
Worship

Printed in the USA
CPSIA information can be obtained
at www.ICGtesting.com
JSHW021415160824
R13664500001B/R136645PG68134JSX00003B/5